FAIRY DUST TALES

# Fairy Dust



BESS ADAMS

PUBLISHED BY WINGS PROPERTIES, LLC
6450 KINGSPOINTE PARKWAY, SUITE 9
ORLANDO, FL 32819

FIRST PUBLISHED IN THE UNITED STATES
BY WINGS PROPERTIES, LLC



THE LIBRARY OF CONGRESS CONTROL NUMBER
2006937049

ISBN 978-0-9790511-0-4
ISBN 0-9790511-0-X

PRINTED IN THE UNITED STATES OF AMERICA

*chapter one*

# true colors

Near a certain town, in a certain forest, on a certain hill, there stood a certain tree. At first glance, there was nothing extraordinary about this tree, except that it stood apart from the others in the exact center of a small grassy clearing. But now, as autumn brought fiery reds and golds to the leaves of the other trees, this one tree seemed not to notice the coming of winter: its leaves were glossy and green, as if it was springtime all year round in this one spot. And indeed, it was.

If you happened to come upon this tree during the dead of winter you would find its leaves bright, and its branches empty of the snow that coated the rest of the forest. The winds never seemed to blow on it, and if you walked under its leaves, you too would feel the warmth of springtime on your face.

As you will have guessed by now, this was no ordinary tree, for the ground on which it grew was fairy ground. A perfect circle of tiny mushrooms surrounded it and, as I'm sure you know, a circle of mushrooms is a fairy circle – one of the most magical places in all the world. Powerful enchantments have protected this spot for thousands of years, and they also protect all the fairies who live there. For inside this very special tree's smooth bark was a whole city, where fairies live, work, play, and go to school.

Now, if you were to look very closely, you might see a tiny, perfectly round knothole near the very top of the tiny door. This knothole was fitted with a tiny round door, no bigger than a quarter. The face of the door was covered with delicate beautiful carvings of many animals – a dolphin, a bear, a unicorn, a cat, and a tiny thrush with its wings outspread – all surrounding a little doorknob in the very center. The doorknob too was carved to resemble the head of an owl. Once inside this door, the outside world of forest and sky disappeared, and an extraordinary new world appeared: a world that, at this particular moment, was anything but peaceful.

Down a long spiral stair in the trunk of the tree, and through a door leading to a winding corridor along a central branch, was another door that opened into a small circular room. In this room, which to you and me would be no bigger than a hatbox, there were five tiny creatures in grey robes pacing back and forth across the floor. Actually, fairies don't really pace, as their legs don't touch the ground – they flutter. But as they were very very nervous, they might as well have been pacing.

These five young friends were waiting, barely able to breathe in their fretfulness - waiting for the door on the other side of the room to open. Cerulia, a small creature, was staring at the floor, every few moments pulling her black hair behind her dainty ears. Rosalinda flitted about letting out deep impatient sighs each time she changed direction. Saffron chewed on her fingernails fiercely as she watched Astarte doodle circles of varying sizes in a small notebook. Vera was the only one who waited patiently with her eyes glued to the door. When that door opened, they would know their fate. There was no escape. This was it - the moment they had feared for so long.

Each of these five girls had known the other since they were baby fairies, when they were barely able to flutter, much less fly. They had played together, gone to school together, laughed and told secrets together. And for the last year, they had been rigorously training together. And now…

With a loud click and an ominous creak, the door opened wide. All five heads snapped up, all ten eyes focused on the figure standing there, framed in the heavy doorway – Madam Moonstone!

Madame Moonstone was the most formidable and most feared teacher at Fairy Dust Academy. Nobody knew how old she really was, but she had been the school's Head Dustmaster for as long as anyone could remember, and that was a long time. Her hair was silver and severely styled around her dark, almost hypnotic eyes, slightly turned-up nose, and tiny, pinched mouth. It was rumored that she had been one of the most beautiful of all the fairies and, even at this moment, when her face seemed to the girls to be cloudy and ominous, anyone could see the beauty that lay just behind those eyes. The girls all held their breath and avoided her gaze.

She fluttered sternly into the center of the room. "Circle, please!" she commanded, in a voice like a trombone, dark but melodic. The girls did as she asked (if asked is the right word) and instantly formed a perfect circle around Madame Moonstone as they had done many times before. You see, fairies never stand in lines, like you and me – they always stand in circles. Effortlessly, Madame Moonstone flicked one wing and began to spin in a slow circle, catching and holding each girl's eyes before rotating to the next. The terror each girl felt was multiplied ten times over as they faced the news that awaited them.

At last she spoke again. "You have all succeeded," she said simply.

The five fairies' dread evaporated in a flash! They were about to scream with joy when Madame Moonstone raised her hand.

"BUT… " The girls' terror was back just as quickly as it had left. Madame Moonstone continued.

"You all just managed to squeak by in passing your final fairy exams, and while many of your teachers felt that you did quite well in your classes, there are many who are not at all convinced that you are mature enough for the responsibilities that come with fairy magic."

Once again Madame Moonstone turned to face each of the girls in turn. "So, you will all remain on probation until you have proven yourselves." The girls gasped. This was unexpected.

"Since I have been your principal teacher, I shall continue to be your mentor and watch over your training until are truly ready. We begin today."

Their hearts sank. Cerulia's eyes again went to the floor while Saffron's fingernails went again to her teeth. More school? They had all hoped to take their first journey outside the tree that had been their home for so long and visit humans!

"But Madame Moonstone," Rosalinda blurted out, unable to contain herself any longer, "why..."

"Hush, Rosalinda!" interrupted Madame Moonstone, her eyes flashing. "This is not a time for questions. You and your friends are very talented." She softened slightly. "Special, I might almost say. I have no doubt that in time you will all do remarkable things in the human world. But with the power of Fairy Dust comes great responsibility. It's not as easy as it might seem in books. You must be careful-"

"Madame!!"

Madame Moonstone broke off her lecture as the door burst open. A strange creature hurtled in, nearly tripping over its own long arms in its haste (and its clumsiness). It was Madame Moonstone's servant, a bad-tempered little goblin who looked like an enormous wart with legs. His name was Grock, and though he was one of Madame Moonstone's most trusted helpers, no one else could stand him. The girls almost simultaneously jerked back just a little.

"Madame," Grock said again, "so sorry to disturb you, but the alarm bells are going off like mad all over the human world. There seem to be disturbances in every single community! Could there be some kind of war going on?"

"No, no," said Madame Moonstone calmly. She smiled slightly to herself. "I should have expected this, as it happens every year at this time. Well, as usual, we'll just have to improvise."

"But Madame," said Grock, "what could possibly be causing such terrible unrest? Is it the beginning of the end??" Grock always had a tendency to make mild unrest seem like Armageddon.

"For many a young girl, that's what it feels like," she replied. "It's the beginning of SCHOOL."

"M-Madame?" said Vera, brushing her very curly, dark-brown hair away from her impossibly large eyes. Madame Moonstone looked up sharply as she spoke. "C-can we help?"

The five girls, almost forgotten as Grock had burst in, now stood with their hands clasped together, their own situation all but forgotten. Somehow they managed to gather strength from each other, and as they stood facing Madame Moonstone, they seemed to grow in stature and confidence. Madame Moonstone, who a moment ago was about to scold the young fairy for her impertinence, now examined each fairy, moving her eyes from face to face, surprised at what she saw. "Well," she thought to herself, "maybe there's more here than meets the eye. Do I dare?"

"Please, Madame Moonstone," said another fairy, who managed a quick smile under her wavy blond hair, "you've taught us well, and I'm SO sure we could-"

"Hush, Saffron," said Madame Moonstone sternly, but she secretly smiled at her earnest young students. She feigned a look of annoyance, then once again barked, "Circle!" The girls instantly obeyed.

"All right then, we'll have to turn your probation into a test case. I'm going to give you an assignment in the human world." The girls again were on the verge of erupting into whoops of joy when Madame Moonstone held up a hand.

"We fairies have a most difficult and delicate work to do," she explained. "Young human girls pass through a period when they are no longer children, but are not yet grownups. It is a very dangerous time, when everything they know about themselves is changing, and they don't know where to turn for confidence and guidance. That's where we come in.

"It is only during this time that we Fairy Dust fairies can be seen, and when the power of Fairy Dust is at its strongest. Children see elves, pixies, gnomes – all that sort of thing. But fairies become visible as you truly begin to grow up, and no longer are a child. Sometimes fairy magic is the only way."

"But Madame," asked another of the girls excitedly, "does Fairy Dust really make magic? I thought it only changed how humans think and feel about-"

"Thank you, Astarte," Madame Moonstone interrupted back. "You are right. The right recipe of Fairy Dust can help a young girl understand her world, and give her strength and courage to make decisions. But our magic can't change things. That's something everyone must do for themselves.

"So now, and quickly too, it's time for you to rid yourselves of those drab grey robes, and for you to discover your true colors. For each of you from this moment onward will have a true color, which is your destiny as a Fairy Dust fairy. Each color of Fairy Dust contains certain properties, emotions, and abilities. When you come to understand how your true color works, you will then be able to mix it with other Fairy Dust colors to create recipes for any circumstance. But always remember, without the belief of the human, Fairy Dust is no different than common dust. Now, stand very still, clear your minds, and we will determine your true colors."

The girls could hardly contain themselves, for this was the moment they had been waiting for all their lives – finally they would learn their true colors! They knew each color of Fairy Dust was special, and that the combination of different colors into beautiful rainbow patterns was how Fairy Dust recipes were created. And now… now it was their turn. They stood stock still in their perfect circle and tried to clear their heads of the swirling and excited thoughts that filled them.

Madame Moonstone took out a tiny crystal vial from her robe, and held it up. At first it seemed completely empty, but the emptiness seemed to twinkle and flash when caught by the light.

"This is clear Fairy Dust," said Madam Moonstone. "It has no color or properties, but as I sprinkle a bit over each of you, it will reveal your true colors. First, Saffron!"

The young, golden-haired fairy gulped in fear as Madame Moonstone faced her. She glanced quickly around at her friends and, as suspected, all eyes were glued to her.

The silver-haired Dustmaster took a pinch of the almost-invisible Fairy Dust and tossed it straight up into the air. Then, she quickly spun around and, with a few perfectly placed beats of her wings, she had covered Saffron in unseen dust. Everywhere the dust touched Saffron, a color instantly appeared, then began to spread out like ripples in a pond, until the young fairy was glowing – YELLOW!

"Yellow is then your true color, Saffron," said Madame Moonstone. "It is the color of trust, of confidence and friendship. Use it wisely – friendship is a very powerful thing." Saffron's eyes moved slowly over her arms as she took in the new yellow glow. A smile grew wide over her face as she repeated the words in her mind - trust, confidence and friendship.

"Next," Madame Moonstone continued and fixed her gaze. "Astarte!"

Astarte held her breath, looking tiny and terrified, as Madame Moonstone repeated her actions, first tossing the clear Fairy Dust into the air, then expertly blowing it towards Astarte with a flick of her wings. Instantly color began to appear covering Astarte in – PURPLE!

"Purple is then your true color, Astarte," said Madame Moonstone. "It is the color of inspiration, of creativity and style. Use it wisely but sparingly, my dear – a little creativity goes a long way!" Astarte, thrilled to be rid of the drab grey robe spun quickly around trying to make sure every inch of her was covered in the beautiful new shimmer.

"Next, Vera!"

Vera shook her curly hair off her face and braced herself as once again Madame Moonstone performed the ritual. She closed her eyes, and when she opened them again she found that her grey robes had disappeared and instead she was covered head-to-toe in – GREEN!

"Green is then your true color, Vera," said Madame Moonstone. "It is the color of affection, of empathy and passion. Use it wisely."

Vera let a small smile make its way across her face as her green glow mingled in the room with Saffron's yellow and Astarte's purple. "Passion," she thought to herself, "I like that."

"Next, Rosalinda!"

It was Rosalinda who had spoken up first, and she hoped her impertinence wouldn't affect her true color. She waited as patiently as she could, then began to see spots

begin to cover her body. She gasped with anticipation and delight – the spots were decidedly – PINK!

"Pink is then your true color, Rosalinda," said Madame Moonstone. "It is the color of courage, of strength and discipline. Use it wisely."

"Cool!" Rosalinda shouted. Although she could feel Madame Moonstone's stare of disapproval at her outburst, she kept her eyes fixed on her changed features.

Madame Moonstone sighed softly and continued. "Next and last – CERULIA!"

Little Cerulia was never the first to speak or act, though in many ways she was the smartest of all the girls. She blinked rapidly and cleared her mind, ready to receive her destiny. Madame Moonstone rapidly covered her with the clear dust, and bit-by-bit she found that she was – BLUE!

"Blue is then your true color, Cerulia. I expected as much," said Madame Moonstone. "It is the color of judgment, of truth and common sense. Use it wisely and carefully, my dear. The world can never have too much common sense. Now…"

Somewhere in the tree a bell rang sharply. Madame Moonstone quickly looked at Grock. "Madame, please – there's no more time!" he pleaded.

"Yes, Grock, you're correct – there's no more time. Come with me, my new Fairy Dust fairies! The world of the humans awaits!" She hurried off through the open door, and was quickly followed by flashes of yellow, pink, purple, green, and blue.

chapter two

# an anything but ordinary morning

Bells rang, clanging loudly in the darkness. Big bells, tiny bells, chimes, bongs, jingles and dings filled the black night. The bells became louder and more frightening by the second, seeming to take away all space and time until nothing was left but darkness and the ringing, ringing, ringing of the bells, like something out of a scary movie. The bells came out of the darkness, sounding the alarm, the alarm, the alarm, the alarm…

"The alarm!" A skinny arm swung through the air in a well-trained arc, landing squarely on top of the snooze button. The bells instantly ceased. In the growing dawn the face of the alarm clock read 6:00am. Amber opened her eyes.

"I hate mornings," she thought, as she dragged herself out of bed and slouched sleepily down the hall to the bathroom. She closed the door behind her and crept up to the mirror, afraid of what she might see.

The face that appeared in the mirror looking back at her was that of a groggy, tousled eleven-year-old, with unruly blond hair and large, green eyes that seemed to change color with her mood (and Amber Duncan was plenty moody enough to give her eyes quite a workout). Her skin was pale and clear but she investigated it closely in the mirror. "No zits today!" she cheered to herself, and then turned sideways, rolled back her shoulders and stuck out her chest. She stood in front of the mirror, anxiously searching for signs of any development, but her profile was skinny and straight as a stick. "Nothing today," she sighed and slumped once more over the sink. "Just another day, like every other…OMIGOSH!!"

Amber froze in her tracks as she remembered – today was NOT like any other day! Today was the day when tryouts would be held for the school play! They were doing a big musical called Anything Goes. It was an old musical, and Amber didn't know anything about it except that there was plenty of dancing. That was all she needed to know.

She loved to dance, and being on stage was one of the few times when she didn't feel awkward or clumsy. She actually felt confident and coordinated, even pretty, when she danced. She had gone to dance class ever since she was four years old, and was pretty good, even if she said so herself. But auditioning, dancing in front of the drama and music teachers, and being judged was something that made her bones freeze. "I'm gonna need some luck today," she thought to herself. "Or better still, some magic."

Amber turned on the shower, threw off her nightclothes and quickly stepped inside, letting the warm water splash all over her. She let out a big sigh and was in the middle of vigorously washing her hair when, without any warning, the water turned icy cold.

"Aaaaaahhhhh!" she shrieked, jumping out of the shower and almost slipping on the wet bathroom floor. She stood there dripping and shivering, her hair and eyes full of shampoo and soap. After a few seconds, she reached back in to see if the water had warmed up again. It was still freezing cold – the hot water was gone.

"What do I do now?" thought Amber. "My hair is full of soap and I gotta look good today for the audition!!"

She grabbed a big comb and began frantically running it through her hair, squeezing as much shampoo as she could out of her hair and into the sink. She could tell that it was still full of soap, and when it was dry it would be stiff and crusty. She pulled it back into a ponytail and hoped for the best.

"Why does this stuff happen to me?" she grumbled out loud as she put on her school uniform skirt and blouse. This was one of the few times she was actually glad that her new school had uniforms, for she knew if she had to choose what to wear today she would still be standing in front of her closet when the sun went down. By the time she gobbled down the piece of toast and orange juice that her mother had left out for her, she was already late and could feel her hair beginning to stiffen into a helmet on her head. She grabbed her books and sullenly made her way out the door to walk to school.

Amber, her mom and her little brother Charley had moved only a few weeks ago and were still adjusting to their new life in the suburbs. For the first ten years of her life, they had lived in an apartment in the middle of a big city and she missed it terribly. There was always something exciting going on, and everything was close by. She loved her school, had a fabulous group of friends, and even had the interest of a very cute boy. But all that was in the past now. After her dad had moved away, her mom told her they couldn't afford to stay in the city anymore, so they found themselves in a boring little house, in a boring little neighborhood, on her way to a boring school. Now she had to start all over again – trying to fit in and make new friends in a brand new world. She felt like some kind of alien on a strange new planet, alone and out of her depth.

Worst of all, this had to happen just as she was changing. She knew she was about to begin growing up, becoming a teenager and, more importantly, becoming a woman. She was excited and terrified, knowing that she was no longer a little child, but not yet grown up. She was a tween, no doubt about it.

And nobody seemed to understand or pay any attention. Her daddy was gone, her mom didn't seem to have time for her any more, and Charley… well, Charley was a baby and a boy, so what did he know? It felt to Amber like she was beginning one of the most important journeys of her young life completely and utterly alone.

Dragging her backpack along as she rushed to make it to her first class on time, Amber saw other girls walking along in twos, threes, and clumps, cheerily laughing and talking together, which made her feel even more alone. She knew she would make friends sooner or later, but right now, all she could feel was her hair rapidly turning to cardboard as she walked along.

But today she had a chance to shine! She started to get excited about the upcoming tryouts for the play. She knew she was a good dancer and couldn't wait to show her classmates and teachers what she could do. Her confidence began to return as she imagined herself in a beautiful costume, twirling gracefully onstage in a spotlight as the audience cheered. She smiled to herself and imagined taking her bow as cute boys threw flowers at her feet. She giggled as she saw herself giving autographs at the stage door. She saw herself walking off holding hands with a boy she had noticed in class the day before. What she didn't see was the tree directly in front of her.

WHAM! The next thing she knew Amber was sprawled on the ground, books everywhere, with a painful lump on her forehead where she had collided with a maple tree that was just shedding the last of its leaves. She pulled herself together as quickly as she could, scrambling to throw her books back in her bag and stand back up as if nothing had happened. She prayed that no one had seen her, but her hopes were immediately dashed as she saw a group of girls across the street pointing and giggling at her clumsiness.

"Some dancer!" she thought to herself. "I can't even dance around a tree without crashing into it. How am I going to make it through an audition? I am such a loser!" All of the confidence she had had a moment ago was gone now, and she felt like a stupid, awkward little baby who didn't even know how to walk, much less dance. Her head was pounding and she could feel a serious lump raising on her forehead. She had grass stains on her new uniform from the lawn where she had fallen, and her backpack was in complete shambles. And now she began to feel the ponytail on the back of her head stiffening up like a beaver's tail, slapping back and forth.

Amber ran the rest of the way to school and barely made it to her locker before she burst into tears. Everything was going wrong! She was supposed to be entering into the most wonderful time in her life and she was messing everything up. She wanted to run, to fly away from school and hide forever. She stood in front of her unopened locker, the warm tears streaming down her face, and felt like a big baby, wanting to be held and hugged and comforted. Then, suddenly, a new thought came into her head, one she had never had before.

"I'm NOT a baby!" she said to no one in particular, as she angrily wiped her eyes. "I don't want to be a child any more. I have to grow up! I just don't know how to do it. I wish I had some help!"

As she spoke these last words, something very strange happened. Amber felt a breeze on her face, which began to swirl around her. The breeze spun itself into a little whirlwind, blowing stronger and stronger around the astonished girl, blowing bits of paper and a few leaves up into the air. As she stood dumbstruck, an even stranger thing happened – a flash of bright blue materialized, then vanished! Then a flash of pink replaced the blue, then yellow, then green, and finally a shimmering swath of purple appeared before her. What was happening?

The air seemed to spin tighter and tighter around Amber. Then, most surprising of all, it headed straight for her locker! As suddenly as it appeared, the whirlwind passed through the vents in her locker door, disappearing inside. Suddenly there was a sharp crack from inside the locker, and a tiny voice was heard saying "Ouch! Get off me, Saffron!" Tiny lights in many colors flashed from inside the locker, then everything was still.

Amber stared, dumbstruck, unable to move, at her locker door. What just happened? This was turning out to be anything but an ordinary day!

Suddenly, a bell began to ring. The first class would be starting in just minutes! Amber gulped hard, then cautiously reached forward and dialed the combination, and even more cautiously, opened the door.

chapter three

# first meeting

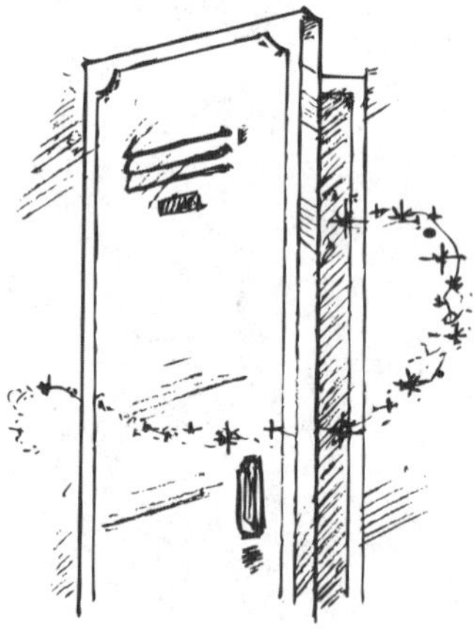

"CIRCLE!" whispered Cerulia as the door began to swing open. They had only just arrived in Amber's locker and everyone was in disarray. As it was the very first time any of them had traveled to the human world, the journey had been anything but smooth.

You see, just as fairies stand in circles instead of lines, they also travel in circles called spinners. You've probably seen a spinner or two yourself in a garden or walkway.

Suddenly, a gust of wind swirls up with no warning, blowing around in a circle as it travels across the ground, and a moment later, it is gone. (Next time you see one, look closely, and you just might see the colored shimmer of Fairy Dust). All of the girls had studied spinner-travel in school, but only Saffron had really been good at it. She twirled light as a feather within the swirling funnel of air, and sometimes even showed off, doing back flips around the others. Astarte, on the other hand, would get dizzy almost immediately, and burst into fits of light-headed giggles, throwing the spinner off-course, careening away from its target. Cerulia, who had the best head for math and was usually in charge of navigation, would wince every time she heard Astarte start to squeal. It was an act of sheer luck that all five fairies landed inside Amber's locker, and not in Gilda Swain's locker next door, which was full of candy wrappers and smelly gym clothes.

As Cerulia compensated for one last shriek of laughter from Astarte, the five fairies were hurled into the dark locker. Vera found herself wedged between two well-chewed pencils, while Rosalinda skidded to a stop, just missing a pot of shimmery lip-gloss. Saffron flitted gracefully to the top of the locker and perched on an empty coat hook while Astarte, still giggling, landed upside-down on a geometry book with Cerulia right beside her.

"Circle! Quick!" Cerulia whispered again. In a flash the five friends flitted to the center of the locker, hovering in a vertical ring like the face of a clock, and nervously faced the door as it creaked open.

The door stopped moving. Outside, Amber had frozen as she heard what sounded like tiny voices coming from inside her locker! Had somebody booby-trapped it? She'd hardly had time to make any friends at her new school, much less enemies. Nobody even knew she existed. Maybe Tommy Fazio, the perennial troublemaker of the eighth grade, had put a mouse in her locker! Whatever it was, something was definitely moving around inside.

Meanwhile the first period was about to start, and almost everyone else had left the hallway. Amber knew she had to open the door – time was running out before Mrs. Steinway, the school Principal, would be out patrolling the halls searching for stragglers. She took a deep breath and quickly pulled the door open.

No matter what she thought she might be facing as she looked inside, nothing could have possibly prepared her for what she saw.

Amber's eyes nearly popped out of her head. There, in front of her, hovering amongst books, paper, and a half-eaten sandwich from yesterday's lunch, were five tiny winged girls, each no more than two inches high, floating in a circle of rainbow colors and looking right at her!

"Hello, Amber Duncan!" said five tiny voices in unison. "We're the Fairy Dust fai-"

Amber slammed the locker door closed and stood frozen in a state of utter bewilderment. She felt her head where she had slammed into the tree – a nasty bump was forming. "That must be it. I smacked my head so now I've got spots before my eyes or, well, tiny people before my eyes." She took a deep breath and pinched her cheeks hard. "Shake it off, Amber! You've got to get to class."

Once more Amber dialed the combination and carefully opened the door.

"Hello, Amber Duncan!" said five tiny voices once again. The little girls were still there in mid-air, smiling at her. "We're the Fairy Dust fai- "

Clang! The door slammed shut again.

Inside the locker, Rosalinda crossed her arms and let out a heavy sigh. "Well! This is going great!"

"She's probably just scared," Vera said.

"Why would she be scared of us?" Saffron asked. "We're here to help."

"Yes," Vera said, "but she doesn't know that yet."

"Vera's right," Cerulia chimed in. "Just give her time."

Just then the door swung open again and the five fairies, startled a bit, stood pin-straight and once again announced themselves.

"Hello, Amber Duncan!"

"I'm going nuts!" Amber thought as she started to slam the door.

"Amber Duncan, wait!" a slightly annoyed voice sounded in her ears. "Please, don't shut the door again."

Amber froze and her eyes popped open. There, hovering just to the right of her nose, was a tiny creature with sparkling pink wings. Her short hair was angled softly around her cheeks and sharp chin and the chestnut brown color was interrupted only by a striking blond streak at the front. Amber's eyes met Rosalinda's and Amber saw a smirky smile sneak across Rosalinda's face.

Amber was petrified. She didn't know whether to run screaming down the hall, or to lash out and try to squish the little pink fairy who, after all, was no bigger than a dragonfly. But the more she looked at Rosalinda smiling at her, the more she felt strangely calm, as if going insane was a perfectly ordinary thing to do.

Just then Saffron zoomed up next to Rosalinda.

"Chill!" Rosalinda said out of the side of her mouth and grabbed Saffron's arm gently. She once again addressed Amber who was now starring wide-eyed at Saffron's brilliant smile. "Hello Amber Duncan. I'm Rosalinda," she said slowly.

"And I'm Saffron," Saffron said as calmly as she could manage.

Next Astarte flitted up. "I'm Astarte."

"And I'm Vera," Vera said as she approached.

"And I'm Cerulia," Cerulia completed the circle and the fairies all looked at each other and said in unison,

"And we're Fairy Dust fairies!"

"Wh-what's a Fairy Dust fairy?" Amber asked, trying not to explode with curiosity and excitement.

"We're here to be your friends, Amber Duncan," Vera said softly and with a reassuring smile. "You called for help, and here we are. Fairy Dust fairies come to the human world especially for girls like you." Vera was keeping to the greeting she had been taught to speak at school and was trying to be as sincere as possible. The first moment of contact between fairy and human was known to be a highly unstable moment for both, and there were many techniques taught at Fairy Dust Academy to help defuse the danger.

Amber's fear began to evaporate. She thought she had heard about Fairy Dust fairies before. Once when she was little, she had peeked into her cousin Emma's bedroom and seen Emma sitting on her bed, deep in conversation with…nobody! Emma was sitting, intently staring at a spot on the bed in front of her and Amber had strained to hear what she was talking about. When she asked Emma about it later, she had grabbed at a silvery necklace around her neck that sparkled with many colors and told Amber that she was talking to her fairies. When Amber had asked if fairies were like imaginary friends, Emma had laughed and told Amber she was too young to understand. This memory came rushing back to Amber as she stared at the five tiny faces before her.

Now Saffron, unable to contain herself any longer, spoke up.

"That's right, Amber Duncan! There are five of us, and we will be here for you as long as you need us. How can we help you?" Saffron was bursting to say more – here she was face to face with a real live human for the very first time – but she managed to stick to the script.

"How come you keep calling me 'Amber Duncan'? It's just 'Amber'," she blurted out, startling the circle of fairies. They looked confused – all except Cerulia, whose eyes brightened along with her smile when Amber confirmed what she had suspected.

"I knew it!" said the blue fairy excitedly. "Just the first name, same as us!"

Cerulia turned to face Amber now. "Hello Amber, my name is Cerulia. I hope we'll all be friends."

"H-hello," said Amber. She blinked really fast a few times just to make sure they were not going to disappear. Nope. All five creatures were still there, still smiling. "So, you guys are fairies? Honest?"

"Honest!" chirped Astarte brightly. "But not just any fairies – we are graduates of the Fairy Dust Academy!"

"That's right," added Rosalinda. "We're here to help you with the power of Fairy Dust."

"Fairy Dust? What's Fairy Dust?" asked Amber, finally able to speak. "Is it magic?"

"Miss Duncan!" a large voice boomed. Amber froze and her heart leapt out of her chest. It was the Principal, Mrs. Steinway, standing not ten feet behind her. Amber slowly turned to face her. Mrs. Steinway was very aptly named, for to Amber she seemed to be about the size of a grand piano. Everything about her was huge, from her hammy hands and her stout legs, to her impossibly plump lips. Only her eyes were small – two tiny slits in the middle of an ocean of face.

"First period has begun, Miss Duncan," Mrs. Steinway continued, full of sarcasm. "I don't know how things were done at your previous school, but at my school that means you should be sitting at a desk in a classroom at this very moment. Now, whom are you talking to? You know cell phones aren't allowed in school."

Amber's brain sounded the alarm. The Fairy Dust fairies were in plain sight, still in their ring around Amber's face, and staring curiously at this new human. Mrs. Steinway would surely see them…then what? Amber's heart began to sink below her knees. But strangely, Mrs. Steinway just stared at her. If she had any awareness of the Fairy Dust fairies, she wasn't letting on. Was it possible? Could it be that only she could see the fairies?

Thinking wildly, Amber decided to take a chance. "Uh, well, um, I'm just kinda talking to, um, myself, Mrs. Steinway. You see, the school play tryouts are this afternoon and I'm just working on a speech for the audition, and…"

"Astarte!" called out a tiny voice.

Amber broke off in a panic as she saw Astarte. The purple fairy had become fascinated with Mrs. Steinway, only the second human she had ever seen, and had broken away from the rest of the group, flitting up to Mrs. Steinway's enormous face. The hair on Mrs. Steinway's head was pulled back into a tight bun revealing two small ears and large dangling earrings. Astarte stared at the sparkling jewelry mesmerized, then, in a quick movement, zipped around to the back of Mrs. Steinway's ear. Amazingly Mrs. Steinway still made no notice of the fairy, but slowly moved toward a stock-still Amber.

"I would suggest, young lady, that you quickly move along to your first period class, or there'll be no reason for you to audition, as your afternoons will be full of detention. You're new, and I'll let you go this time, but…what are you smiling at?"

By this time Astarte had all but climbed into Mrs. Steinway's ear. She of course was completely oblivious, but Amber could hardly control herself from bursting out laughing. She quickly looked at the floor and regained her composure.

"Don't cross me young lady," snorted Mrs. Steinway, her ear still full of fairy. "Now hop to it!"

"Yes, ma'am," said Amber meekly, still not daring to look up at Mrs. Steinway, but imagining Rosalinda popping out of the other ear, Cerulia reclining on her bottom lip, Vera dancing in the pile of hair and Saffron sitting neatly on the bridge of her steel-rimmed glasses.

Mrs. Steinway's footsteps echoed down the hall as Amber rushed back to her locker, opened it and grabbed her books. She knew she had just escaped from serious trouble. Suddenly the ring of fairies appeared in front of her again.

Astarte was giggling to the other fairies, "Wow! Humans are loud, aren't they? And so big! And did you see that? There were sparkles growing out of her ear!" Finally she turned her attention back to Amber, who seemed shaken by the whole encounter. "Oh, tell us about the play, Amber!" she said with a giggle.

This was the last straw. Scared first by teeny tiny colored bugs, then almost getting detention just before the tryouts, and the bump on her head still throbbing Amber felt exhausted and defeated.

"Look," Amber addressed the fairies, "I'm having a terrible morning and if I don't get to class I'm going to be in big trouble. I don't know if I can believe any of this, but right now all I know is you're in my way so please, please, please just get lost, okay?"

Amber ran down the hall, trying to keep from crying. It didn't work, and by the time she got to class, her eyes were burning with tears.

The five friends watched her go down the hall. She finally turned a corner and disappeared, her angry footsteps fading into silence. They looked at each other sheepishly, trying not to cry themselves.

"Did she say…did she say she didn't believe?" Saffron asked, trying to keep the panic she felt out of her voice.

"No," Cerulia spoke up quickly, "she said she didn't know if she believed."

"Well," said Vera quietly, "that didn't go too well, did it?"

chapter four

# fairy dust

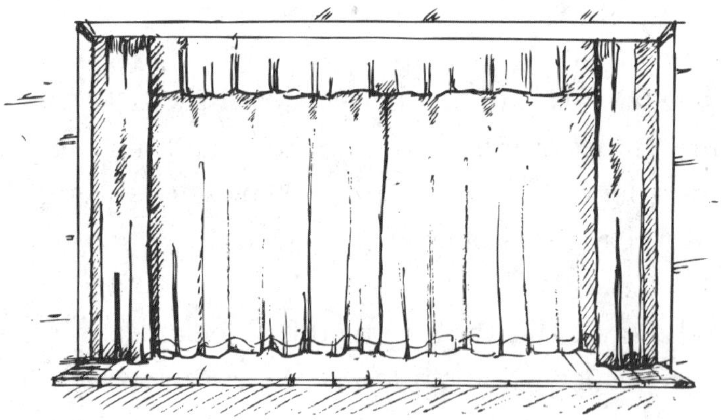

The school day passed in a blur for Amber. During morning classes she was all but comatose on the outside, while inside her head was spinning a million miles an hour. *There are fairies in my locker!*

At lunch she ate by herself. She had planned to spend the lunch hour preparing for that afternoon's audition, but even that had been forgotten. *There are fairies in my locker!*

After lunch, in her geography class, a pop quiz sent her into a total tailspin. Geography was one of her best subjects, but she couldn't remember if the capital of Austria was Vienna or Zurich, or if Lapland was part of Holland or Finland. Only one thought kept circling around in her brain, making her dizzy with fear and confusion: *There are fairies in my locker!*

"Why me?" she thought to herself. "Why today? They said I called them, but how did I do that?" Her thoughts swirled back through the day, trying to remember what she might have done for there to be *fairies in her locker*!

Amber sat glumly looking at her half-finished quiz and felt more dazed and confused than ever. Everything about her life was the oddest it had ever been, as if she was wearing someone else's clothes, or someone else's skin for that matter. She closed her eyes and winced as she remembered her awful bone-chilling shower, her crackup with the maple tree, hearing the other girls laughing at her, and finally her unpleasant meeting with Mrs. Steinway. Could today get any worse?

Once again her eyes popped open as she remembered the auditions that afternoon. If only they could happen any other day but today! She knew she could do it – she was good! This was her chance to show everyone what Amber Duncan could do. But how could she remember a dance combination if she couldn't even remember the capital of France?

Finally the bell rang. Amber sadly turned in her paper and trudged out of class, feeling doomed. Her self-confidence was gone and she felt more alone than she ever felt in her life as she made her way back to her locker. "I'm just gonna get my stuff and go home," she thought to herself. "No point in humiliating myself even further. I'll just go home and hide under the bed until I'm thirty."

Once more she stood in front of her locker and dialed the combination. "Suppose those colored bugs are still in there," she wondered. Without warning she banged her fist loudly on the door. "You better not be in there! I want you out!" she yelled. A group of boys who were coming down the hall stopped and stared, then laughed as they passed her. "Oh well," she thought, "they might as well think I'm crazy, 'cause I probably am." She banged again, then put her ear next to the door and listened hard. Not a peep. She sighed, pulled the door open and stopped still in her tracks and stared.

The inside of her locker was neat as a pin: her books were stacked, and even alphabetical, her pencils and pens were all back in her pencil box, the half-eaten sandwich had disappeared, and her hairbrush and barrettes were carefully arrayed. But Amber didn't notice any of this. She was staring at something else.

There, hanging from a hook in the middle of her locker, twinkling silver in the light, was the most beautiful necklace she had ever seen. At the end of a delicate chain, a tiny, silver, winged creature stood at attention in front of a little crystal vial. The vial was filled with sparkling crystals in many different colors. Amber knew instantly what it was.

FAIRY DUST!

Amber's hand reached into the locker and gently touched the necklace. She felt the smooth silver and cool crystal, then let go and watched it sway gently on its silver chain. She also knew that she had seen just such a necklace before – around her cousin Emma's neck many years ago. And now here it was.

Fairies. Fairy Dust. Magic. For her.

It was real!

At that moment she heard the sound of music – the faint tinkling of a piano playing a jazzy tune. Then a girl's voice, echoing down the hall:

"If you're ever in a jam – here I am
If you're ever in a mess – SOS
If you ever get so happy you land in jail – I'm you're bail
That's friendship, friendship
Just the perfect blendship…"

The tryouts had begun! Down the hall in the auditorium, Mr. Conrad the music teacher, Mrs. Ramsey, who taught English, and Miss Jamison the gym teacher were putting would-be singers, actors, and dancers through their paces. The musical they were putting on, Anything Goes, needed a cast that could do all three, and do them well.

"That's friendship, friendship..." sang the voice from down the hall.

Amber remembered something that the green one (what was her name?) had said. Vera! That's right, that's her name. Vera. She said, "We're here to be your friends, Amber Duncan."

Her eyes went back to the necklace and Amber looked more closely at the vial. In it she saw thousands upon thousands of tiny shimmering crystals – blue, pink, purple, yellow and green. Five colors. Five fairies. Five friends?

Suddenly her hand reached forward and grabbed the necklace, but instead of putting it around her neck, she stuffed it into a pocket. She closed her locker, turned around, and made her decision. Then, slowly, she turned toward the sound of the music and walked determinedly down the hall.

If Amber had stayed another few seconds outside her locker, she would've heard a snapping sound, as her pencil case popped open, followed by five tiny moans as five squished fairies poured out of it into the dark locker.

"Whew!" gasped Cerulia. "I couldn't take much more of that! We might have all suffocated!" She flitted up and looked out the vents in the door.

"Which way did she go?" asked Astarte excitedly. "We can't let her down. Madame Moonstone would kill us!"

"Oh stop moaning," said Rosalinda, peeling herself out of the pencil case. "She took the necklace. That's a good thing. Now she just needs to put it on! Which way did she go, Cerulia?"

"Towards the music!" cried Cerulia happily. "She's going to the tryouts! C'mon, let's go watch!" She slipped through the vent and was gone.

"Wait!" called Vera, as she flew after her. The others followed quickly. There was no time and they were far too excited to summon up a spinner, so the five fairies sped off, one after the other, towards the sound of the auditions in the distance.

"This feels so weird," said Astarte as she flew along. "We should be in a circle, not stretched out like this in a…what do humans call it?"

"We're in a line," called Rosalinda, speeding along after Cerulia. And so they were, for the very first time in their lives. Cerulia led the way with Vera, Rosalinda, and Astarte close behind. Saffron, usually a good flyer, had a cramp in her wing from hiding in the pencil box, and lagged behind. The music was getting louder, and now another voice, a boy's voice, was singing a love song.

Faster and faster they flew. They turned to the right and down another corridor until they came to an open door marked "Auditorium". There was a piece of paper tacked to the door that read: Tryouts today! Sign up inside. And there, standing half-in and half-out of the door was Amber!

The five fairies came to a stop high over Amber's head and regrouped into a circle, feeling much more comfortable to be finally out of the line. The last to arrive was Saffron, who had finally managed to stretch out her cramped wing.

"What do we do now?" asked Astarte. "We've got to make her go inside!"

"We can't make her do anything, Astarte, you know that," replied Rosalinda. "She's got the necklace with the Fairy Dust recipe inside. It's up to her now."

"But unless she puts it on, the Fairy Dust won't work!" cried Saffron. "We've got to tell her!"

"No," said Cerulia, holding up her hand. "Remember what Madame Moonstone said. She's got to put on the necklace of her own free will. Only then will she believe in its power. We've got to sit tight and wait."

"Oh, look at all the people! She must be so scared," sighed Vera. "Remember how nervous we felt when Madame Moonstone was grading our flying exams?"

Just below them, out of earshot, Amber stood paralyzed with fear. Inside the auditorium, she could see boys and girls staring at pages of music and scripts. Everyone had to sing first, then they would dance. She saw a couple of girls that she shared classes with, as well as a boy she had noticed from the very first day of school. His name was Eric Tolliver. He was a year older than Amber, with unruly dark hair, sharp eyes, and a really cute smile. It was his voice the fairies had heard singing as they came around the corner… and he was good!

Just inside the room, Miss Jamison, the gym teacher, sat at a table checking people in. She was a tall, skinny woman with short red hair, and a wide thin-lipped smile constantly on her face, even when she was mad. Amber liked her a lot.

"Coming to audition, honey? Tell me your name again. It's Ruby, isn't it?" Miss Jamison smiled.

"Uh...it's Amber, Miss Jamison, Amber Duncan. I... I'm a dancer."

"Amber! That's right. I knew you were a jewel of some sort. You're new this year, right? Well, come on in, honey, and good luck!"

The auditorium was a big room, with folding seats in rows like a real theatre and a raised stage at one end. Amber crept in and sat near the back by herself. On the stage sat an old upright piano, where the music teacher, Mr. Conrad, accompanied Eric Tolliver's song. Mr. Conrad had a big round bald head like a moon, which bobbed up and down as he played. He was very serious, and never smiled at all, which made Amber nervous.

Eric finished singing. A couple of girls near the front broke into applause, which made Eric blush as he went to sit down. Meanwhile the five fairies had flown up above the stage and nestled into the folds of the curtain to watch.

Mr. Conrad sullenly looked around. "Has everyone sung a song?" Slowly, sheepishly, Amber raised her hand.

"Come on down, honey!" called Miss Jamison, far too loudly. "Mr. Conrad, this is Amber. She's new this year! C'mon and sing for us, dear!"

Everyone turned and looked at Amber. As she felt every pair of eyes in the room staring at her, she imagined the bump on her head to be the size of a basketball, and that her hair, still stiff with soap from the morning's shower, looked like a mop on the top of her head. It was all she could do not to run out of the room, but she managed to walk down the aisle, right past Eric Tolliver, and climb the steps onto the stage towards the waiting Mr. Conrad.

Above her head, five tiny voices were quietly cheering.

"This is SO exciting!" bubbled Astarte "GO, AMBER!"

"Sssshhh," whispered Rosalinda. "We mustn't let her know we're here!"

"Oh, I hope she's good. I just know she will be!" said Vera, peering down over the curtain folds.

Amber reached the middle of the stage where Mr. Conrad sat waiting at the piano. "I…I don't know what to sing," she said quietly.

Mr. Conrad patiently nodded. "That's all right, just sing Happy Birthday. That'll be fine. Let's see what you can do." And he began to play.

Amber looked out into the auditorium at all the other kids, waiting to judge her. She took a deep breath and began. Her voice sounded tiny in the big room, but she was on pitch, but just barely.

"Happy Birthday to you,
Happy Birthday to you..."

She suddenly realized she didn't know what name to sing. She panicked, but then just in time an idea came to her.

"Happy Birthday dear Saffron,
Happy Birthday to you!"

Saffron nearly fell out of the curtain overhead when she heard her name.

"THAT'S ME! THAT'S Mmmmpfh..." she shrieked with delight, and the other girls had to clamp their hands over her mouth.

"Very nice, dear," said Mr. Conrad half-heartedly. Amber's heart sank. She knew she hadn't been bad, but she was too frightened and self-conscious to do her best. And nothing but her best was going to get her into the show. She stepped off the stage and passed Miss Jamison, who avoided looking at her. Ouch! Overhead, the fairies sensed Amber's growing terror.

"What do we do? What do we do? What do we do?" Astarte gasped, feeling a bit terrified herself.

"Nothing," said Rosalinda firmly. As much as she wanted to fly down and try to help, she knew it was all up to Amber now.

"Let her sing again! Let her sing again," Astarte continued. "I could fly down and…and hide behind her ear and sing for her!"

"Rosalinda's right, Astarte," said Vera. "We just have to hope she remembers what she has in her pocket." The others glumly nodded. They knew that it wasn't up to them to help the situation – they needed to put their trust in Fairy Dust.

"All right everyone," called out Miss Jamison, "let's dance!"

Sitting huddled in her seat, Amber froze. She knew this was her real chance to show what she could do, but her fear was getting the best of her. All the other kids were climbing up onto the stage to learn the dance combination, but she remained rooted to her chair, her hands thrust deep into the pockets of her uniform.

Then, she felt it. One of her fingers touched a cool, slender bit of chain. Another rubbed against a tiny crystal tube…the necklace! Slowly and carefully she pulled it out and held it up in front of her. It sparkled in the light, the Fairy Dust inside glittering. "What have I got to lose?" she thought to herself. And with that she slipped the chain around her neck.

chapter five

# dancing from the heart

"SHE'S PUTTING IT ON!!!" Cerulia yelled.

The five fairies, hidden in the folds of the curtain above the stage, rushed forward to see, spilling out into mid-air. In their excitement they forgot to fly, and before they knew it they found themselves hurtling in a multicolored streak downwards towards the stage. They all managed to screech to a halt in the nick of time, just inches from Mr. Conrad's shiny bald head, and if you had been there, you might have seen what looked like a halo of Fairy Dust crowning the frowning music teacher as he sat waiting at the piano. They halted there and once again eagerly turned their eyes towards Amber, in the back of the auditorium.

Meanwhile, Amber had indeed taken the Fairy Dust necklace out of her pocket, and slipped the silver chain carefully over her head, and waited. "Okay, Fairy Dust, do your stuff!" she said to herself.

It occurred to her that she had no idea how she was supposed to feel, or what would happen next. As far as she knew she had never had anything to do with magic before. Would it tingle? Or would she feel super-strong, or super-smart, or super...what? She stood, waiting, as the other kids made their way up onto the stage, and began to sweat. Nothing. She felt just as deflated and hopeless as she had after she finished singing. What was wrong?

"She's not moving!" cried Saffron. The fairies were still in a circle above Mr. Conrad's head as he sat at the piano. "Come on. She needs us! There's no time to lose!" Saffron began to fly towards the back of the room where Amber stood motionless and alone.

"Saffron, NO!" shouted Rosalinda. She darted forward and grabbed the yellow fairy by the arm. Quickly the others joined her.

"Rosalinda's right, Saffron," said Cerulia simply. "Remember what Madame Moonstone taught us. We've got to let the Fairy Dust do its work. If we don't trust Fairy Dust, how can we expect Amber to? All we can do now is wait."

Saffron nodded. She knew in her heart they were right. Vera took her hand and together they flew up to the curtains once again.

The rest of the students were now on the stage, waiting for Miss Jamison to teach them the dance combination. Everyone would learn the same dance together, then they would perform it in small groups. Those that couldn't do the steps well enough would be cut. Miss Jamison, smiling as ever, bounded up onto the stage and stood in front or the rows of nervous auditioners.

"All right, then," she chirped. "Is this everybody?" She turned her eyes out into the room, and spied a lone figure in the rear. "Amber, honey, come on! Time to show your stuff. Let's dance!"

Amber looked up, hearing her name, and her eyes met Miss Jamison's. The teacher grinned at her and motioned for her to come up on stage. Amber hesitated, ready to run out of the room, and then something unusual happened. As she stood looking at Mrs. Jamison, the words "Let's dance!" began to echo again and again in her head. Then, Amber did something she hadn't done since she and her family moved away from the city. She began to smile!

"Lets dance," she thought. "Yes! Let's dance!"

Suddenly, her fear was gone, and all she felt was how much she loved to dance, how graceful and beautiful she felt, how confident and alive she was when she was on stage. She nodded to Miss Jamison, and found that she was running towards the front, up the steps, and joining the rest of the kids onstage.

"Look, look, look! It's working!" squealed Astarte from her perch above the stage. The other fairies watched with delight as they saw Amber's smiling face and her bright eyes.

"Now we just have to hope we got the Fairy Dust recipe right," said Cerulia. "The proportions have to be just so. Did everybody measure carefully?"

"Oh Cerulia, relax! Of course we measured carefully!" said Rosalinda pertly. "Madame Moonstone was standing over us the whole time!"

Astarte nodded. "I wanted to add just a teeny pinch more purple, you know? Just to add a little more zing! But Madame Moonstone wouldn't hear of it."

Cerulia fluttered nervously. "I just want this to work. Amber needs this!"

"Well, you said it yourself Cerulia," said Saffron, "all we can do is watch now."

"Look at her, everyone!" cried Vera excitedly "She's going to dance! She's going to do it!" The fairies stopped their chatter and peered out of the curtains again as Amber took her place, and Miss Jamison strode to the front of the group.

The dance audition began, and it wasn't easy. Miss Jamison quickly taught the group a series of steps, kicks, turns, and jumps that left a lot of the kids gasping for air or scratching their heads in confusion. Amber, her eyes focused and bright, carefully learned each step. She was in her element now, and she began to glow, not just with perspiration, but also with excitement, as she mastered each move. Some of the other kids had begun to notice her dancing, and some were even copying her. Miss Jamison turned her way now and again, nodding with satisfaction.

The whole group was practicing the combination together now as Mr. Conrad played the music over and over. One particularly difficult bit involved a running jump to the right. Amber had the steps down cold and was right in the middle of her jump when…crash! The girl who was dancing next to her jumped left instead of right, and she and Amber collided hard in mid-air. Both girls crumpled to the ground as the music stopped and everyone else stared.

"Oh no!" cried Vera. The other fairies gasped. From their perch above the stage, they could see Amber's eyes drain of confidence and be replaced with terror and confusion.

"Nothing to be done," muttered Rosalinda under her breath, hiding her own fear. Rosalinda had been beaming as Amber showed her confidence – confidence was her part of the Fairy Dust recipe. Now it looked like her work had failed.

Amber flashed with anger as she quickly untwisted herself from the other girl. She had done it right, and now she looked like an idiot again! She got to her feet and turned on the girl who was still on the floor – the stupid girl with two left feet – and was about to lash out at her in fury and frustration, when she suddenly stopped.

The other girl was still on the floor. She was small, with dark hair and even darker eyes, which right now were filling up with tears. She looked up at Amber and miserably said, "Sorry," as one tear splashed out of her eyes and rolled down her cheek.

Amber felt herself thinking, "I know just how you feel…like a loser." Instead of anger, all she could feel now was compassion and concern.

Amber stretched out her hand. "It's okay," she said, and to her surprise, she meant it. The girl took her hand and Amber helped her to her feet.

Overhead, Vera swooned with joy. Compassion had been her part of the recipe. It was one of the hardest parts to get right, when so many other strong emotions like anger and fear get in the way.

"Are you all right, girls?" asked Miss Jamison, who had come bustling over, her face full of concern and her mind full of broken bones.

"I think so, Miss Jamison," said Amber. She turned to the girl, who was brushing herself off and wiping her eyes. "Are you okay, uh…?"

"Robin," said the dark-eyed girl. "I…I think so."

"Well Robin, you look a bit shaken up," said Miss Jamison kindly. She had seen Robin make a number of mistakes. "Why don't you have a seat and relax for a bit?"

Robin's eyes welled up with tears again. "Please, Miss Jamison, I can do it! Let me try again! Please?"

"Now, dear," said Miss Jamison, "I think this is just a bit too hard for you."

"She can get it, Miss Jamison. Let me help her."

Robin and Miss Jamison turned and looked with surprise at Amber, who continued. "She's just getting on the wrong foot. I'll bet I can fix it."

Miss Jamison hesitated, and then shrugged. "All right, just try not to land in a heap on the floor again." She moved back to the front. "All right everyone, let's try the dance in groups of six! Mr. Conrad, music if you please!"

Amber grabbed Robin's hand and moved to the back of the stage. There would be a number of groups ahead of them, so they would have time to work.

"You're being very nice," said Robin sadly. "But Miss Jamison's right. It's too hard for me."

"No it's not, you're just leaving out a step," said Amber, smiling. "You can do this. You want to, don't you, Robin?"

"Oh yes!" said Robin, smiling back. "I love to dance… um…what's your name?"

"Amber. Amber Duncan." Now it was Saffron's moment to turn an excited back flip. Amber was making a friend! The power of the yellow Fairy Dust was coming through!

"Okay, Amber," said Robin, smiling for the first time since they had collided. "What do I do?"

"Let's practice the steps one by one, then we'll put them together. I think you're missing a step just before the jump…"

As the rest of the kids performed the dance in groups of six for Miss Jamison, Amber and Robin worked on each step until Robin could do the whole routine. Other kids had sheepishly joined them, and Amber gave out pointers and corrected footwork, spending more time helping others than working on her own dancing. Miss Jamison, from the front of the stage, occasionally looked over and smiled to herself.

Finally it was time to go to the front of the stage and perform. Amber and Robin were in the last group of six. Amber positioned herself up front so that the others could see her. The music started and they began to dance. Amber made sure she did the steps very cleanly and precisely, looking back from time to time to make sure that Robin and the others were doing it right. And they were – everyone in Amber's group had performed beautifully. Everyone that is, except for Amber. She had concentrated so much on everyone else that her own dancing was clean, but not beautiful.

Astarte was beside herself. "I messed up!" she cried. "I knew I should have put in more purple Fairy Dust! She didn't have any style! I failed." Astarte burst into tears and buried herself in Vera's arms. But she was not the only one who saw what Amber had done.

"That was very nice, Robin. I didn't know you had it in you," said Miss Jamison. "But Amber, you danced like you were demonstrating the steps. Come here, please."

Amber's heart sank. First she sang poorly, now her dancing had been boring. She walked up to Miss Jamison, who put an arm around her and took her aside.

"That was a very generous thing you did, young lady. You made sure everyone else looked great, but now it's time for you to shine. Go back up there and do it all by yourself...and Amber, dance from your heart."

Amber was stunned, frozen to the spot. Dance from my heart? What did she mean? Miss Jamison met her eyes, smiled and winked at her, and pushed her out onto the floor. "Mr. Conrad, one more time please!"

The music started. Amber was alone on the front of the stage, and she began to dance. She heard Miss Jamison's voice in her head saying, "Dance from your heart," and she felt her body become light as air. Every step was full of joy, and she began to smile bigger and bigger as she turned and leaped high into the air. All of her love of performing came out and she glowed as everyone else in the room stared at her. Was it Fairy Dust? Or was it the real Amber coming to life? Was this what Miss Jamison had meant?

The music stopped as Amber hit the final pose and the room became still. If you had been there, and if you had listened very carefully, you might have heard the sound of five tiny voices cheering at the top of their lungs high above the stage.

"Thank you, Amber," said Miss Jamison simply, her eyes shining with pride. "And thank you everyone. We will announce the casting tomorrow afternoon. That's it for today."

As the rest of the kids began to leave the auditorium, Robin came rushing up to Amber. "That was awesome!" she said breathlessly. "And thank you. I hope we both get in the show. You're a real friend."

"I hope so too," said Amber, still a bit dazed. "I'll see you tomorrow Robin."

"Let's have lunch together tomorrow, okay?"

"Okay," smiled Amber. As Robin raced off, she realized that no matter what else might happen, she wasn't alone. Was all this because of Fairy Dust?

As Amber left the auditorium many of the other kids smiled at her. She made her way down the corridor, and as she passed a group of boys, she saw that one of them was the boy with the good voice and the cute smile. Eric Tolliver! He looked right at her, flashed a wicked grin, and gave her the thumbs up sign. She turned bright red, and in spite of the feeling that she had melted onto the floor, she managed to continue walking normally.

Finally she made it to her locker and pulled it open.

"HOORAY!!" came the cheers of a circle of tiny voices. The fairies rushed forward and all began chattering at once about the events at the auditions – how well she had danced, what she had done for Robin, even the chance meeting with Eric Tolliver in the corridor.

"He's so CUTE!" squealed Saffron. "I hope he gets in the show too! Does he have a girlfriend?"

Amber just stood there, unable to speak, until the fairies had finally chattered themselves out. Then she slowly drew her Fairy Dust necklace out from beneath her blouse. "Thank you," she whispered.

"Do you like it?" asked the yellow fairy.

"It's…it's beautiful," whispered Amber, finally taking her eyes off the tiny silver fairy and the crystal vial and smiling shyly at the golden-haired fairy, whose wings fluttered and flicked behind her like an excited cat's tail. "You're…you're Saffron, aren't you?"

Saffron was so pleased that Amber remembered her name that she shot up into the air, did a double back flip, then slowly floated down until she was level with Amber's nose. "That's right, Amber Du-," she caught herself as she remembered first name only, then smiled bigger than she ever had in her life. "I am the maker of yellow Fairy Dust."

Amber looked back at the necklace. Inside the tiny vial were hundreds and hundreds of grains of yellow dust, intermingled with grains of blue, green, pink, and purple. She looked back at Saffron, then around the circle to the green fairy.

"And I'm Vera, maker of green Fairy Dust."

"Yes, I remember," said Amber "And purple…you're Astarte. And pink…Rosalinda! And blue…um…Cer… um…"

"Cerulia," smiled the blue fairy. "Thank you for believing in us, and in Fairy Dust."

Amber looked again at the beautiful necklace. She had a million questions and wasn't sure where to start. She also knew she was already late to get home and help with dinner.

"So, what does Fairy Dust do? I just know that when I put it on, I started feeling good. Is it magic?"

"It's a kind of magic," explained Cerulia. "It can't give you super-powers, or make you invisible, or things like that. In fact there's nothing you can do with Fairy Dust that you can't already do."

"Then I don't understand. I felt different! I know I did!"

"It's hard to explain," said Rosalinda. "Fairy Dust helps make things clearer, so you know what to do. We put together recipes using all the different colors of Fairy Dust. Each recipe helps you make good choices, or helps you understand a certain situation. For example, the recipe in the necklace you have on was designed to help you with the audition this afternoon. The pink Fairy Dust helped you have confidence and believe in yourself."

"And the green Fairy Dust helped you to sympathize with the girl who ran into you," added Vera.

"And the purple Fairy Dust helped you dance with your own style," Astarte chimed in.

"And the yellow Fairy Dust helped you make friends with Robin. Oh, I'm so excited you're gonna have lunch together tomorrow!" chirped Saffron.

Amber looked at Cerulia. "And what about the blue Fairy Dust?"

Cerulia came forward. "Blue Fairy Dust helps you understand. It's what you're using right now. All of this is strange and new to you. Many things during the next few years will be strange and new, as you journey from childhood to womanhood. Many things won't seem to make sense. Blue Fairy Dust will help you see the truth in things, and in yourself."

"So this, uh, recipe, was for the auditions today. What happens tomorrow?"

"It depends on what is most important to you," continued Cerulia. "Whether it's concentrating in class…"

"Or picking what clothes to wear…" added Astarte.

"Or making new friends, or meeting boys…" chimed in Saffron.

"Or getting along with your Mom or your little brother…" said Vera.

"Or standing up to a bully," added Rosalinda. "Fairy Dust can help you make the right choice."

Amber was silent for a minute. All of this was so new, so different, so exciting…the events of the day had been crazy. At the end, she had danced with all the joy she knew she had, she had made a new friend, a cute boy had noticed her, and…she had fairies in her locker!

"Thank you," she said finally. "Will I see you tomorrow?"

"You never can tell!" said Rosalinda brightly, and suddenly a gust of wind whirled through the locker, and they were gone.

chapter six

# secret ingredients

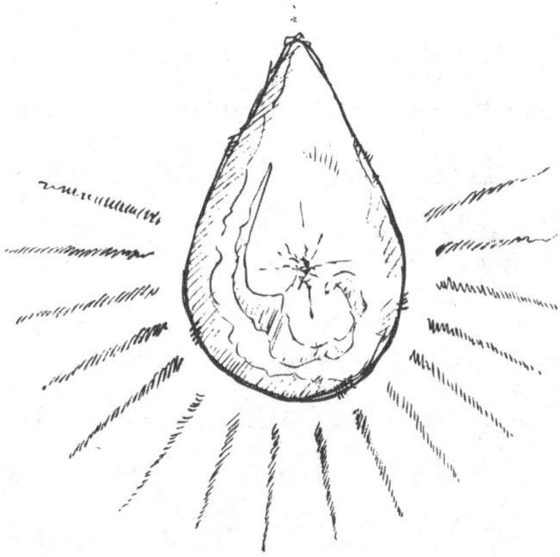

"Disgusting," said a wheezing squeezebox of a voice.

Halfway up a certain tree in a certain forest, inside a long and twisting branch, a small and grumpy creature shuffled along, dragging the knuckles of his scaly hands on the floor as he walked. As he made his way along the hallway, he gingerly picked up a half-eaten birdseed sandwich and the crumbs from a bag of pixie chips, sniffed at them, spat, and stuffed them in a leather pouch.

"Disgusting," he hissed again, louder and nastier than before. "Don't care if they've got their colors – they got no manners."

Grock the goblin was not in a good mood. He hadn't been in a good mood since the five young Fairy Dust fairies had returned from their first mission in the human world. He liked things quiet. He liked things orderly and neat. And these five children had come back to the Magic Tree, screaming and laughing and celebrating their great success as if they had saved the whole world from flesh-eating ogres. Not only were they insufferably happy, they were making a mess all over his nice clean branch.

Grock spied a wrapper from a package of sweet-and-sour sprite snacks and angrily snatched it up. "Madame Moonstone will hear about this," he grumbled to himself, "and then they'll get it!" Just ahead, he heard a shriek of laughter and cringed. You see, goblins are naturally unpleasant creatures, and the sound of happiness is like the sound of nails on a blackboard to you and me.

A door up ahead led to a room in an adjoining branch, and behind this door came the sounds of five very giddy fairies. If you were to imagine what a fairy slumber party might be like, then you would have an idea what was going on in this room. Grock stuck his hairy fingers into his even hairier ears and scuttled down the hall to escape the racket.

"Madame Moonstone will hear about this," he muttered again.

Behind the door was a little room about the size of a loaf of bread. This was the five fairies' common room where Saffron, Astarte, Vera, Cerulia and Rosalinda had lived together since they started classes at the Fairy Dust Academy. Five little doors led to five little bedrooms around the outside, while in the center was a large round fluffy couch, made of the soft tops of dandelions. On top of this cozy nest, the five friends lay on their backs, their wings folded underneath them, and giggled uncontrollably.

It had been two weeks since the day of the auditions, when the fairies first met Amber and gave her their very first Fairy Dust necklace. The next day, Amber found out that she and Robin were both cast in the chorus of Anything Goes. Not only that, but Eric Tolliver, the cute boy with the good singing voice, was playing the lead!

Rehearsals had begun the following week, and Miss Jamison had been so impressed by Amber's dancing that she had given her a solo part in one of the dance numbers. Everything seemed to be going well for Amber – she had lunch with Robin almost every day and was even getting along with her little brother Charlie. She woke up each morning excited to get to school, and every morning, just before she left the house, she took her beautiful Fairy Dust necklace from her dresser drawer, kissed it, and slipped it over her neck. Whether it was magic or not, she didn't care – she was happier than she had been in a long, long time.

The fairies had been able to see it all from the comfort of their dandelion couch. As they lay in a circle in the middle of the room, they could look upwards and there hung an enormous dewdrop, clear and round and shimmering, hovering over them like a watery crystal ball. At this moment, its glassy surface reflected the room and the five fairies like a funhouse mirror, making their smiling faces seem larger and distorted. But then, as they watched, their images faded away into a pearly white glow, and suddenly they saw Amber! It looked as if she could see them too: she was staring straight at them with a happy smile upon her face. But then her face came closer and closer, until her puckered lips were all they could see. A moment later the image flew up, then finally came to rest facing the door, which opened, and on they went down the stairs and out the front door.

As you have probably guessed by now, these pictures came from the Fairy Dust necklace itself! You see, the eyes of the little silver fairy holding the crystal vial were enchanted, and could actually see, as long as someone who believed in the power of Fairy Dust touched the necklace. As soon as Amber took the necklace out of the drawer, her five fairy friends could watch everything that happened to her. The fairies never missed a morning, for they loved the feeling that each time Amber kissed the necklace, she was actually kissing each one of them!

The silver dewdrop on which they watched Amber's daily adventures is called a vista-sphere, and is as normal in the fairy world as a television is to you and me. The vista-sphere is an invaluable tool for looking after the human world from a distance: Fairy Dust fairies can check to see if a particular recipe is working and, if their help is needed, they can hop on a spinner and be there in an instant.

The vista-sphere in the fairies' room would only show images from a necklace that held their recipe, so Amber's necklace was the only 'channel' available to them. However, away above them in a private chamber, the Dustmaster had a very powerful vista-sphere that could tune into any Fairy Dust necklace in the human world. Not only that, she could tune into any vista-sphere, so that at this very moment, as our fairies shrieked, giggled, and dropped even more pixie chips on the floor, Madam Moonstone was observing them, frowning.

"Ah well, it's to be expected," she sighed to herself. "They're young, and this is their first success in the human world. But if they expect Amber to grow up, they have some growing up of their own to do."

At that moment the squat figure of Grock burst into her chamber, wheezing and hissing. "Madame!"

Madame Moonstone raised a hand to quiet him. "Yes, Grock, I know – they're behaving like children."

"Spoiled children Madame – they should be taught a lesson! Little brats…I'd like to…"

"That's enough, Grock!" said Madame Moonstone sternly. "I believe teaching lessons is my job." She looked at the little goblin. He was sputtering with rage, but knew better than to answer back.

Madame Moonstone sighed again. "Every time it's the same, and no one knows that better than you! A new group of Fairy Dust fairies returns from their first mission, they become addicted to watching their success on the vista-sphere, they laugh and scream and make a mess. You should be used to it by now, my long-armed friend."

Madame Moonstone smiled at the ugly little goblin, whose anger slowly subsided. She really did like him, disagreeable as he was, and he was invaluable as the caretaker of the Magic Tree. Grock, for his part, was very fond of Madame Moonstone, though he thought she was far too lenient with her students. He believed in strict rules and harsh punishment, as all goblins do.

"The main thing is, what will they do next?" wondered Madame Moonstone, turning her attention back to the vista-sphere. "Amber has responded wonderfully to the

Fairy Dust recipe. Rosalinda, Vera, Saffron, Astarte, and Cerulia have created their recipe correctly and with care. They have made Amber believe in them, and in herself. All that is very, very good. But now, what is the second recipe? That is where the danger lies."

"What do you mean, Madame? What danger?" asked Grock.

"Never mind, Grock," said the Dustmaster. "We'll just have to watch and see."

Back in the common room, the fairies had their eyes glued to the vista-sphere. They had watched Amber arrive at school and had squealed with excitement as each new person greeted her. Amber had made a number of new friends in the last few weeks, and she and Robin had become really close. Now Amber and Robin were walking together towards their first class, talking excitedly about the new dance they would learn at that afternoon's rehearsal. Suddenly they came face-to-face with a pair of dark eyes and a cute, lopsided grin. It was Eric Tolliver. The fairies gasped and stopped chewing.

"Hi Robin. Hi Amber," said Eric, a little shyly.

Amber was speechless. She tried to stammer out a 'hello', but could only manage a strangled 'huu'. Robin fortunately came to the rescue.

"Hi Eric! Gosh, aren't rehearsals fun? Today should be great. We're doing the big number at the end of Act One!"

Eric hadn't taken his eyes off Amber even as Robin chatted away. "Yeah, it'll be fun. You know, it's the first time we'll be on stage at the same time."

Amber nodded, and once again said, "Huu."

"You know Amber, you're a really good dancer," continued Eric. "Maybe we'll get a chance to dance together this afternoon. See you later." Eric smiled again, and he was gone.

"Huuuuuuu," said Amber once more, but none of the fairies heard her. They were all screaming at the top of their lungs, as junk food flew everywhere.

"HE LIKES HER! HE LIKES HER!" shrieked Saffron.

"Oh wow, oh wow, oh wow!" stuttered Astarte.

"Amber ROCKS!" yelled Rosalinda

"I just LOVE him!" swooned Vera.

"Wait a minute! Wait a minute! WAIT A MINUTE!" shouted Cerulia. Everyone else slowly stopped and stared at the blue fairy.

"What's the matter with you, Cerulia? Don't you think he's gorgeous?" asked Saffron tartly. The other fairies giggled.

"Stop it!" retorted Cerulia, with a look of concern on her face. "Nothing's the matter with me – it's what's the matter with Amber!"

"What are you talking about?" asked Astarte.

"Didn't you see her? Didn't you hear her? She couldn't even look at him, and all she could say was 'huuu'. It was a disaster!"

Rosalinda's head jerked up. "Cerulia's right! All of her confidence was gone! The Fairy Dust must be wearing off!"

"She needs our help," cried Vera "She must feel awful!"

"I know! I know!" said Astarte brightly. "It's time for a new Fairy Dust recipe. A recipe for LOVE!"

"YES!" Saffron squealed. "That'll be so exciting! Then we can watch them fall in love on the vista-sphere!"

"Wait!" Cerulia spun in a circle and waved her arms in the air to get their attention. "We don't have a recipe for love! That's not part of our training. After all, girls this age are too young to fall in love."

"Well, we'll just have to get creative then, won't we?" said Astarte, brightening at the prospect of designing something brand new. "After all, we've proven that we can do this, and we've passed all our courses, Amber trusts us..."

"That's right," said Vera. "We've proved ourselves with a standard recipe. Now let's show Madame Moonstone what we can really do!"

"But..."

"No buts, Cerulia," said Rosalinda. "We're all in this together! Amber needs us, and we're going to get her a boyfriend! Agreed?"

Rosalinda thrust her hand into the center of the circle.

"Agreed!" said Astarte and placed her hand on top of Rosalinda's.

One by one the others did the same. Finally, Cerulia shrugged and laid her hand on top. "Agreed!" she said, and the pact was complete.

"So where do we start?" asked Saffron.

Astarte had already begun to hatch an idea. She turned to Saffron. "With you, of course! We start with the best friendship recipe we can find. Then we just…spice it up a bit! And I've got just the thing – hang on!" Astarte rushed into her room, and the others could hear her rummaging through her closet.

"Friendship! Of course!" said Rosalinda. "Then we add a little extra pink Fairy Dust for confidence…"

"And a dash of extra green, for more passion!" Vera giggled.

Cerulia shook her head. "I…I don't think we should be altering…"

"Come on, Cerulia," interrupted Saffron. "We made a pact, remember?" Cerulia was silent. "Now what else?"

"A little of this!" said Astarte, emerging from her room. She carried a brightly colored bit of cloth, which was wrapped around a small slender object. She slowly unwrapped the cloth, revealing a soft, silver braid, which seemed to give off a radiant glow. It was beautiful.

"What is it?" asked Cerulia excitedly, her misgivings now forgotten.

"It's a lock of a unicorn's mane," whispered Astarte, "one of the strongest love charms in the world!"

Everyone stared at the sparkling silver strands. They had all heard about the magic of a unicorn's mane, but none of them had ever seen a unicorn before, much less a lock of one's hair. Unicorns themselves had all but disappeared, though rumors of sightings were common.

"But it's so rare. Where did you get it?"

"My grandmother gave it to me," smiled Astarte. "She told me that there would come a time when I would find it useful. I guess that time is now."

"But how do we know how much to use?" asked Cerulia. "Shouldn't we talk to Madame Moonstone?"

"This is our pact," said Rosalinda abruptly. "It's our recipe. Astarte, what did your grandmother tell you about how to use it?"

"Well, she said never to touch it – that even holding it was incredibly powerful. We should use the tiniest strand of hair, and put it into our Fairy Dust vial along with the recipe."

"How exciting!" cried Saffron. "Unicorn mane, mixed into our Fairy Dust!"

"All right," said Rosalinda, "there's no time to lose! We need to create the recipe, put it in a new Fairy Dust necklace, and get it to Amber before the afternoon rehearsal. Let's go!"

They raced to the door, yanked it open, and flew down the hall, almost trampling a little creature that had been standing in the hallway outside. It was Grock, who coldly watched them disappear down the winding branch, and then turned to survey the mess they had left in the common room.

"Disgusting!" he muttered once more.

chapter seven

# recipe for disaster

"Huuuuu..."

Amber stood, slack-jawed and wide-eyed, in the middle of the hallway. Other students rushed by as the first period was just about to begin. Some of them stared or giggled as they passed. Amber didn't hear or see them, (or anything else for that matter). She just stood in total shock, brainless and motionless, in the midst of a hive of activity.

"Amber, snap out of it! What's wrong with you?" Robin waved her hand in front of the dazed girl's eyes, and gave her shoulders a shake. Slowly Amber's eyes came back into focus, as a little goofy grin began to appear on her face.

"Hi Robin. What's up?" Amber smiled at her friend. Suddenly the bell for class rang. The sound seemed to bring Amber back to reality, and her face froze in panic as she remembered her meeting with Eric.

"Oh wow, oh wow, oh wow!" cried the wide-eyed girl, sounding surprisingly like Astarte had just a few minutes before. She grabbed Robin's hand with a mixture of elation and terror. "He…he wants to dance with me! What do I do? What do I do?"

"If I were you," boomed a voice from behind the two girls. They froze at the sound. Mrs. Steinway! The girls whirled around to face the enormous presence of the school principal.

"If I were you," Mrs. Steinway repeated, as a tiny smile appeared on her huge face, "I would get to my first class this instant, or the only dancing you'll be doing this afternoon will be in detention. Now hop to it!"

Robin and Amber didn't need to be told twice, they each sprinted off in different directions to their first classes.

For the rest of the day Amber did her best to concentrate, pushing away the events of the morning and trying not to think about the rehearsal that afternoon, when she would see Eric again. But she couldn't help smiling to herself and imagining what it might be like. And every once in a while, her hand strayed up to her neck and her fingers clutched the vial of Fairy Dust that hung there.

It had been a long time since she had seen the fairies, but she still vividly remembered that day and how her life had seemed to change since she had put on the Fairy Dust necklace. In fact, up to today she had almost always felt relaxed and confident. But now…she couldn't help the feeling of panic when she thought about the coming afternoon. She felt shaky, even trembling, and for the first time wondered if the magic of the Fairy Dust might be wearing off. She missed the fairies. Would she ever see them again?

It was with these thoughts in her mind, and confusion beginning to take over her whole body, that she made her way to her locker to stash her books before the start of the afternoon's rehearsal. She dialed the combination, half-hoping that she would hear five tiny voices calling, "Hello, Amber Duncan!" when the door opened. But her locker was silent. With ever-increasing anxiety, she tossed her books inside and was about to slam the door in frustration when a beam of light reflected off something shiny, and she saw it.

There, once again, suspended on the hook, was another Fairy Dust necklace! Twinkling in the light at the end of the delicate chain, the little silver fairy guarded a vial full of brightly colored crystals. Amber took off her necklace and compared it to the new one. Immediately she could see that the colored dust was arranged differently and in different proportions – a new Fairy Dust recipe! And, if Amber had looked very close, she might have seen a single slender white hair woven in among the Fairy Dust. The fairies had added a tiny strand of unicorn mane to their improvised formula.

Without thinking twice, Amber took the new necklace and thrust it in her pocket and left the old one hanging in her locker. She smiled for the first time since that morning and dashed off for the rehearsal, excited and hopeful.

"She's got it!"

Astarte, who had been dutifully watching the vista-sphere since the fairies had returned from placing the necklace in Amber's locker, excitedly gave the call. The other four fairies came rushing out of their rooms and assembled under the glowing silver sphere. But, to their surprise, there was nothing to see but blackness.

"What's wrong?" said Cerulia crossly. "Is there a problem with the reception?"

"She put it in her pocket," answered Astarte. "She's on her way to the rehearsal now!"

"Oooh, this is soooo exciting!" giggled Saffron, hugging a pillow made of peach fuzz. "And it's our very own recipe. Madame Moonstone will be so proud if us!"

"Or she'll kill us," said Rosalinda, half-meaning it. "I hope this works."

"Oh, I have a very good feeling about this," cooed Vera. "Everything we did was based on an approved recipe for 'emotional connection, strong friendship, and honest expression'. We just improved it a bit."

"You and your feelings, Vera! It's the unicorn mane that has me worried," chimed in the ever-practical Cerulia, biting her lip. "We just don't know how strong its effect will be."

"Will you lighten up, Cerulia?" said Astarte, rolling her eyes at the others. Her eyes caught something moving on the vista-screen. "Here we go! Look!"

Sure enough, the picture had brightened and they could see images swirling and swinging by. Amber was taking the Fairy Dust necklace out! They could see the auditorium, and the stage, where a few pieces of half-painted scenery had appeared. Kids were milling about, getting ready for the rehearsal to start. Mr. Conrad the music teacher, scowling as ever, sat behind the piano. Miss Jamison was nowhere to be seen yet. Then all of a sudden, Amber's face filled the screen, her eyes bright with excitement. All of the fairies cheered, then braced themselves as Amber's lips kissed the tiny silver fairy holding the vial, just as she did each morning. The fairies let out one big collective sigh, then, as they did every morning, they all cried out, "Okay Fairy Dust, do your stuff!" and settled down excitedly to watch.

Amber slipped the necklace over her head. "A new necklace. A new Fairy Dust recipe!" she thought to herself again. She then dashed up to take her place on stage. Today they would learn the dance for the act one finale of Anything Goes, and everyone was in it, even Eric. And maybe, just maybe, they would actually dance together!

That thought made Amber dizzy – very dizzy. The room started to spin and she could feel her heart racing. She tried to calm herself down, and took a few deep breaths. Slowly the room righted itself again, and she was able to see clearly. Across the stage Robin was waving at her. The two friends rushed together and hugged. They hadn't had a chance to talk since Mrs. Steinway interrupted them that morning.

"Amber! You look funny. Are you okay?" Robin asked.

"I'm fine, just a little dizzy, that's all." Amber rubbed her eyes, shook her shoulders, and took a deep breath. "I guess I'm just excited."

"I guess!" giggled Robin. "I would be too after what Eric said this morning!"

At the mention of Eric's name the room once again swirled in front of Amber's eyes, and she almost fell to her knees. But at the same time she felt happy and light, as if nothing could go wrong. She smiled broadly as she regained her balance. Robin looked at her curiously.

"Are you sure you're okay, Amber? Why are you smiling?"

"Of course I'm okay, honestly," shot back Amber. "Let's dance!"

At that moment Miss Jamison sailed into the room and up onto the stage. Both Robin and Amber had liked Miss Jamison right off, and they liked her even more with every rehearsal. She always had a smile and an encouraging word, even when things were going badly.

"Helloooo, everyone!" she crowed. "Let's get started! We have a lot to learn this afternoon! Please take your positions where we left off yesterday."

The setting was supposed to be the ballroom on an ocean liner. There was a wide set of steps in the middle of the stage with a platform at the top and a railing going down each side. Amber and Robin had been at the top of the steps when they had finished yesterday, so they made their way to their positions, each against one of the railings. Everyone else scrambled into place, until the whole picture was assembled.

"Perfect. Very good!" smiled Miss Jamison. "Now remember, this is a very swanky dance, and everybody is dressed in tuxedos and evening gowns. It's very romantic!"

"Romantic," murmured a smiling Amber, a little too loud. A few people near her raised their eyes, and a couple of the girls giggled. Miss Jamison either didn't notice, or pretended not to.

"So," said Miss Jamison, "when we finished yesterday's rehearsal we were up to Eric's entrance. Where is Eric?"

Once again, as Eric's name was mentioned Amber's head swirled and felt light. As much as she denied it to Robin, she did feel odd. But at the same time, she felt good – warm and sort of gooey inside. Her heart sped up every time she heard Eric's name and she couldn't stop smiling!

"Eric," sighed Amber, loud enough for everyone to hear.

"Yes?" said a voice. Amber turned her head toward the sound and then froze as she saw a tall tousled figure in the doorway. It was Eric! Amber gasped – had he heard her? She tried to compose herself but could not stop smiling.

Eric didn't seem to notice. "Sorry I'm late, Miss Jamison," he said, quickly setting his backpack down and coming up on stage. "Where do you want me?"

"Thank you for joining us, Mr. Tolliver," said Miss Jamison sarcastically. "Top of the stairs please, between Robin and Amber."

Amber let out a little shriek and her grin got even bigger and goofier. What was happening? Robin slid over and grabbed her arm. "Get a hold of yourself!" she whispered to Amber, and pinched her hard. Amber jumped and her eyes cleared for a second, in time to watch as step by step, Eric came closer and closer, until he was standing at the top of the stairs between them.

"Something's wrong," whispered Vera, her eyes fixed on the vista-sphere. She couldn't see Amber's face, but she could sense from Amber's voice and the others' reactions that something wasn't right.

"Oh don't be so negative, Vera," said Saffron. "It's just getting good!"

The others shushed them both and stared excitedly at the screen. Eric was standing right next to Amber!

Amber had managed to clear her head as Eric approached. This was her chance, she thought, her chance to show Eric how talented and mature she was. Eric turned to her.

"Hi Amber," he said and smiled.

Amber's head began to swim again and her heart was beating like a kettledrum, but she managed to hold onto her composure long enough to say hi back.

Miss Jamison began to teach everyone a series of complicated steps full of little jumps, turns, and changes of direction. Amber and Robin were both able to learn them easily and Eric was surprisingly good dancing between the two girls. As Amber danced next to Eric, she could feel herself beginning to grin uncontrollably again. As she looked at Eric, she imagined herself as Miss Jamison had described, looking beautiful in a gorgeous evening gown. She turned to Eric and saw him dressed in a top hat and tails. It was all so romantic! Eric smiled at her and she fluttered her eyes, flirting shamelessly with him. Something was making her lose control of her composure. Part of her felt wonderful and free and crazy, while another part was in a total panic.

"Wonderful! Wonderful! Well done!" beamed Miss Jamison. "Now lets put it all together with music. Ready Mr. Conrad? Here we go…five, six, seven, eight…"

The music began and everyone started to dance. Amber felt herself smiling bigger and bigger. She was in her own world now. The whole stage had transformed into the ballroom of the ship, and Mr. Conrad and his piano had transformed into a whole orchestra. Everything she saw was beautiful, and everyone was dressed like an old Fred Astaire movie. And she was Ginger Rogers!

Suddenly she broke away from what Miss Jamison had taught, making up her own steps and twirling around, showing off for Eric who was staring at her wide-eyed as he tried to do the proper steps. Robin had all but stopped, staring. Miss Jamison finally looked up to the top of the staircase and gasped.

"Miss Duncan! What are you…"

But it was too late. Amber was now totally in her own

world, leaping and dancing and swirling around Eric, who had stopped dancing and stood in shock.

"Amber, stop!" whispered Robin, but Amber couldn't hear her. She had started singing along with the music she heard in her head. By now, everyone had stopped dancing and stared, but Amber just grinned and danced. And then…

"Dance with me, Eric," sang Amber, and she grabbed the stunned boy and began to dance with him around at the top of the stairs. Amber was now laughing wildly, holding onto Eric tighter as he followed along in utter shock. Mr. Conrad stopped playing, and the room was silent and still as everyone watched Amber go completely insane.

"Amber, please stop!" Robin couldn't stand it any longer. Her friend was in trouble! She rushed in between Amber and Eric, pulling the two apart and holding on to Amber. Amber struggled to break free, laughing and singing all the while. Robin held on tight, but Amber was too wild. She swung an arm backwards, catching Robin full across the face with the point of her elbow. Robin fell backwards, tripped, then plunged down the stairs, landing in a heap at the bottom, motionless. Everything was still.

Amber stopped and stared, as if she had awoke from a dream. Miss Jamison ran to Robin, knelt beside her, and turned her over. The dark-haired girl moaned, coughed a little, and then opened her eyes.

"I…I'm okay," said Robin shakily. Miss Jamison slowly helped her to her feet. No one else had moved. But slowly, all the eyes in the room turned toward Amber.

In another room, in another place, five tiny pairs of eyes watched in disbelief.

"Oh wow," whispered Astarte. "Oh wow, oh wow."

"What have we done?" whispered Rosalinda.

Amber stood stock still at the top of the stairs, too mortified to move. What had she done? Eric stood just a few paces away, unable to look at her.

"I think Robin will be fine," said Miss Jamison quietly. The room heaved a collective sigh of relief. "And I think the best thing for everyone will be to get right back in the saddle and continue our rehearsal. However, Miss Duncan…"

"I'm so sorry, Miss Jamison," came a tiny voice, almost unrecognizable as belonging to Amber. "I don't know why I…" she trailed off.

"We'll talk about it tomorrow, young lady," said Miss Jamison, in the sternest voice she had. "Right now, I think it's best if you go home."

"Yes, ma'am," Amber slowly climbed down the stairs, gathered her books, and left the auditorium. Only after she had made it down the hall did she allow herself to cry. And cry she did – big sorrowful sobs that rained tears down her face, and onto her cheeks, dropping onto her necklace.

Her necklace.

Fairy Dust!

She stopped still, and her fingers grabbed the vial on the end of the silver chain, lifting it to her face. She stared at it, and in her mind she saw the little silver fairy stare back. And it seemed to laugh at her. Her eyes narrowed. It must have been the Fairy Dust! The unhappiness she felt began to harden into anger. Those fairies! Those bugs! They did this to me!

Anger turned to rage. She had lost everything. She was a laughingstock! She could never hold her head up in school again. She was a loser!

The tears came again. She slowly took off the necklace, its pretty silver fairy and bright colored dust glistening as if nothing had happened. She balled it up in her hand, and threw it at the ground. The tiny vial shattered, and the little silver fairy skittered away across the floor. Amber walked away and left it there.

A moment later something else happened – something Amber didn't wait around to see. All the thousands of brightly colored crystals began to fade, slowly turning from bright pink, green, blue, purple, and yellow, into a dingy, lifeless grey.

For that is what becomes of Fairy Dust that no one believes in.

It becomes dust.

chapter eight

# mushroom detail

"CIRCLE!" said a voice like an angry trombone.

Saffron, Vera, Astarte, Rosalinda, and Cerulia jerked themselves up and out of their stupefied trance. They felt terribly weak, and had trouble breathing, as if there was no air left in the room. They barely managed to flutter into a ragged circle.

They had just witnessed the most horrible thing imaginable to a fairy: they were no longer believed in. For a fairy, being believed in was like food and drink to you and me – it is a necessary part of life. Without belief, a fairy will die, fading away just as the bright colors faded from the Fairy Dust scattered on the floor at Amber's school, ready to be swept away by the janitor's broom. Indeed, as they looked at each other, sick with fear, they could see that their own colors seemed to be fading. Rosalinda seemed more ashen than pink, and Saffron's yellow was more of the color of putty. They looked at each other in disbelief, unable to utter a word.

The door to the common room flew open, startling them. But it was not Madame Moonstone whose voice had called them into a circle, it was Grock. He was smiling a smile that could only be described as evil, and his red-splotched eyes glinted with glee. And if that wasn't enough, he smelled awful.

"Done something we shouldn't have, haven't we girls?" he hissed through jagged, yellow teeth.

Grock stepped into the room towards the terrified fairies. They all instinctively shrank back from him, trying to hold their circle. Where was Madame Moonstone? Grock took another step and began to chuckle hideously. That was all the poor girls could stand. They suddenly screamed with one voice and scampered towards their rooms, but before they could get to safety, the five doors of the five rooms suddenly swung shut with a bang!

"Going somewhere, girls?" came the gurgling voice again. Grock's eyes became narrow and hard. "I don't think so!" He slammed the hall door behind him and took another menacing step towards the fairies.

"That's enough, Grock," said another voice, coming from the center of the room. The little goblin hissed his displeasure, but retreated.

From above, the vista-sphere came to life. First, a pair of glowing eyes, beautiful but angry, appeared in the middle of the orb, then the rest of Madame Moonstone's striking face came into view. She seemed to be looking in every direction at once, for each of the fairies could see the furious Dustmaster looking straight into her eyes.

"I believe I said circle if you please!" boomed Madame Moonstone. The five fairies lurched forward and managed to re-form into a circle. Then, as the girls stared in wide-eyed astonishment, the head in the vista-sphere floated towards the bottom of the ball, then emerged into the room! First her head, then her neck, shoulders, torso, and legs – Madame Moonstone materialized out of the vista-sphere in front of them, her eyes blazing, and her wings flitting threateningly. She flicked one wing and slowly turned, facing each fairy in turn.

"Am I angry? No, I am incandescent with rage!" said the Head Dustmaster, her voice remaining calm. "You have broken no less than fourteen rules of Fairy Dust policy and procedure, including the use of a non-Dust substance in your improvised concoction, which I will not dignify by calling a recipe! And, if I am not completely mistaken, that substance came from an endangered species, one deserving of our help and protection. Am I not right, Miss Astarte?"

Astarte, already pale, turned white as a sheet. "We…we just wanted to help Amber, Madame Moonstone," she stammered. The other girls nodded.

"Help her?" asked Madame Moonstone smoothly. "Help her? I see. And I suppose your idea of helping her is to have her humiliated in front of her friends and classmates, and to lose her newfound belief in herself, and in you. Is that it?"

Rosalinda cleared her throat. "We started with an approved recipe Madame, really we did! We just tried to…"

"Improve it? Yes, Rosalinda I can just imagine! You are all so clever, so headstrong. You had one success, and decided that you could do better than all the books, all your teachers, and all the many hundreds of years of Fairy Dust practice! And Amber! Were you thinking about her? Or just about yourselves?"

The room was silent. No one could answer Madame Moonstone, or even look at her. Finally, after a long pause, Vera meekly looked up.

"We're so sorry, Madame Moonstone," she whispered through her tears. "We did the wrong thing. What can we do to make it better?"

Madame Moonstone's eyes softened for a moment. "Well, that's the first sensible thing any of you have said for some time," she said. Then her eyes flashed again. "The first thing you will do is be punished for your misconduct, using that poor human girl as a guinea pig. Grock!"

The goblin bowed low, delighted to be part of the fairies' punishment.

"Take them down to the cellar. They will be on Mushroom Detail until further notice. And while you work, think about what you have done, and what you must do to make things right. Now go!"

Without another word, Madame Moonstone rose up towards the ceiling, and before any of the girls could do more than gasp, she was swallowed up into the vista-sphere once more, and with one last flash of her eyes, she was gone. The five fairies turned to face Grock. Mushroom Detail. None of them had the slightest idea what that was, but from the eager look on Grock's face, they knew they weren't going to like it.

"Follow me," said the goblin, with a gleam in his eye.

Grock led them out the door, along a passage, and down a winding stair they had never taken before. Down, down, down they went, through the massive trunk of the tree, right down into its gigantic roots. As they descended, the air became thicker, warmer, and more humid, and they began to sweat. They wanted to slow down, but Grock kept up a furious pace down the stairs. It felt to them like they had been spiraling down for hours. By the time they reached the bottom, the five dejected fairies were drenched, their hair hanging limply down and their clothes sticking to their backs. Grock turned to them and grinned his yellow-toothed grin.

"In here," he said, and walked through a low opening carved out of an enormous root. Meekly, the five girls followed him, ducking their heads to pass through the doorway, and found themselves in a dimly lit room. The low ceiling was dark and brown, and the floor was packed earth. It was impossible to tell in the low light just how big the room was, but it seemed to go on forever in all directions. There was a musky, damp smell hanging in the humid air.

"What is this place?" Astarte asked as her eyes adjusted to the dim light.

"It looks likes a dungeon," said Cerulia, a little frightened.

"It smells like a dungeon," said Saffron pinching her nose.

"Are you sure that's not Grock?" Rosalinda whispered and they all let out a little giggle.

"This is punishment," Grock hissed as a wicked smile grew on his face. The fairies fell silent and the smiles faded from their faces.

"It's about time you children learned," Grock continued, "you can't just do as you please all the time."

Grock cleared his throat with a disgusting sucking sound and slumped out of the room. The five fairies were alone in the endless room. They surveyed their surroundings and saw raised patches of earth, with walkways in between, like an enormous checkerboard. Each patch of earth was about three inches square, and they seemed to go on forever. In the center of each patch, the girls could make out a little white dot, the size of a pea. Everything was very still and very quiet.

"Where do we start?" asked Vera after a pause.

"And what's Mushroom Detail?" added Saffron, adjusting her footing on the damp floor.

Cerulia could not hold herself together any longer.

"Well thanks a lot, Rosalinda!" she cried, looking as angry as her tiny features would let her. "You and your pact!"

"Me? It's Astarte's fault!" Rosalinda retorted hotly. "It was her idea to add the bogus unicorn mane!"

Astarte was hot with anger. "BOGUS? What do you mean, bogus? Cerulia's right – you bullied everyone into doing this and now we're all in a lot of trouble!"

"Come on you guys!" said Vera, stepping into the middle of the circle. "This isn't going to help us!"

“Oh shut up Miss Goody-Goody!” sneered Rosalinda. “A fat lot of good your green dust did! What does green Fairy Dust do, anyway?”

“Well, I didn’t want any part of this anyway,” sniffed Cerulia. “I told you it wouldn’t work and you never listen to me!”

“Oh, get over yourself, Cerulia!” said Saffron, who had been smoldering while the others argued. She flew at Cerulia until they were nose-to-nose. “What makes you think you’re so smart? Who do you think you are – Mini-Madame-Moonstone? Hah!” Saffron tuned her back and flitted away.

That did it. Suddenly they were all nose-to-nose, screaming, pointing fingers, and shoving each other. All of their anger, frustration, and humiliation came pouring out as they fell to the ground fighting. Soon their sweaty clothes and faces were caked in dirt, so that it was no longer possible to see what their true colors were.

“Waaaaaaaaa…” came a sound from somewhere deep in the room. It was faint, but very high-pitched and piercing.

“Waaaaaaaaa…” came another, its sound jarring with the first. Then a third, and a fourth.

The girls' ears pricked up at the sound, and they came to a halt to listen, with hands still clutching hair and legs, entangled like a large brown blob in the middle of the floor.

"Waaaaaaa! Waaaaaa! Waaaaaaaa!" More cries came now, surrounding them. Each sound was tiny by itself, but as ten, then twenty, then thirty high-pitched wails overlapped and repeated, the overall effect was very powerful.

"What is that awful noise?" asked Astarte. The others looked around in the dim light. Some of the sounds seemed very close by, others echoed off in the distance. But there was no doubt that every second more wails could be heard. Hundreds now. Then thousands. The sound was piercing and unpleasant making it hard to think. And with every second, it got louder and louder.

"Look!" called Vera, who had untangled herself from the rest and stood up, dirt crumbling out of her hair. She pointed to one of the nearby patches of raised earth. The little pea-sized white dot in the center of it suddenly shivered, then started to move!

The other fairies jumped to their feet.

"Over there!" cried Rosalinda, as another dot began to move.

"And there!" gasped Cerulia, looking in a different direction.

More and more of the little pea-sized dots squirmed, and shivered and stretched in their beds of earth, and more and more wails filled the air. Terrified, the girls tried to plug their ears, but the sound was too strong. It was coming from the dots! They stared as one of them shook from side to side, and then began to slowly raise itself up, revealing a slender white stalk underneath.

The fairies froze. They knew where they were. And with one voice, they all whispered, "Mushrooms!"

Now they could see that each of the little white dots was the cap of a little mushroom, and as more of them stretched their caps upward, they could see that each cap sat on a tiny stalk. There were hundreds of them!

"We're in the baby mushroom beds," gasped Vera. And so they were.

As you no doubt remember, the Magic Tree sat in the middle of a perfect circle of mushrooms – a Fairy Circle. These mushrooms act as sentinels, guarding the enchanted circle. In fact, all mushrooms do! Whenever you see a mushroom popping up in the middle of a garden, or a lawn, or a forest, you will know that fairies are nearby. Deep in the roots of the Fairy Tree are the baby mushroom beds where mushrooms live until they are old enough to go on duty. They spend most of their time sleeping in their little earth beds, getting bigger and stronger tucked in tight to the ground. But if they are disturbed, they become just like all babies - they get upset and squirm and cry, until they are comforted back to sleep.

All of the babies were awake now, crying with their piercing little cries, squirming and thrashing in their beds. The fairies watched in horror as one of the mushrooms pulled itself out of the earth and began wriggling and screaming. Then another, and another!

"This is awful!" yelled Saffron, trying to be heard above the racket. "What do we do?"

"It's our fault they all woke up," cried Vera "It was our yelling and fighting."

"What?" shouted Astarte. "I can't hear!"

"Circle!" yelled Rosalinda, almost in a panic. "Close together so we can hear!"

The girls formed a tight circle, facing each other shoulder to shoulder. Meanwhile the whole room was now in an uproar, with unhappy howling baby mushrooms wriggling all over the floor.

"We made this mess and we've got to fix it," yelled Rosalinda.

"Cerulia, you're the smartest," cried Saffron. "What do you remember about mushroom care?"

"Oh, now it's okay that I'm smart, huh?" yelled Cerulia, still stinging from Saffron's taunts.

Saffron bristled. "Fine! If you're going to be that way about it…"

"Stop it! Please!" pleaded Vera. "We've got to work together!"

"Vera's right," Astarte added. "There's only us and these screaming mushrooms, and we're running out of time!"

Saffron and Cerulia looked at the others, then at each other.

"I'm sorry, Cerulia," said Saffron. "I just get jealous of you sometimes, you know? 'Cause you are smart. You're the smartest fairy I know."

"I…I'm sorry too," Cerulia stammered and blushed pinker than Rosalinda's wings. "A-and you're the prettiest fairy I know."

"That's all wonderful," Rosalinda interrupted impatiently, "but it's time to do something!" They were surrounded now by white thrashing babies. They seemed drawn to the fairies and some had even squirmed into the circle. The sound of their cries was earsplitting.

Saffron asked again, at the top of her lungs, "Cerulia, what should we do?"

The blue fairy thought hard, trying to picture all the books she had read on fairy plants and magical helpers.

"Well, they're really a lot like regular babies, if I remember right."

"We don't know anything about regular babies," said Astarte, "and I certainly don't know anything about magical plant babies."

"I know! They need lots and lots of sleep," Vera recalled.

"That's right," Cerulia affirmed. "Babies have to sleep almost all the time."

"Yes, but they're awake now!" shouted Rosalinda. "How do we get them back to sleep?"

Cerulia thought again. Then it came to her. "They have to be given comfort," she said simply. "And love."

"Comfort and love? How do we give comfort and love to baby mushrooms?" asked Saffron.

"I don't know," said Rosalinda, "But we've got to try!"

The pink fairy picked up a wriggling infant that had wrapped itself around one of her legs, held it out at arms length, and began making shushing noises at it. The poor little mushroom responded by screaming so loud Rosalinda almost dropped it! Vera took the baby from Rosalinda, and tried holding it close and stroking it. At first it seemed to be working, the suddenly the baby shrieked and squirmed out of her grasp! Astarte caught the little mushroom before it hit the ground. She began to bounce it up and down, singing a little fairy song. As if by magic, the little baby stopped crying, and within seconds it was fast asleep.

"That's one," sighed Saffron.

It wasn't easy. The fairies found out early on that none of them could do it alone. There was no one single way that would work for all the baby mushrooms. So the five girls worked together, fanning out through the space, trying to decide whose strengths would work best with each crying baby. Vera patiently held the fussiest ones, listening until they were cried out or softly humming them lullabies. Astarte found the babies that wanted to play and came up with games that would calm them down and wear them out until they fell back to sleep. Cerulia tried her best to remember everything she had ever read about babies – mushroom and human – and tried a number of different methods to calm them, from rocking them to holding them upside down. Saffron and Rosalinda gathered a bunch of the mushroom babies together and told them stories about Fairy Dust Academy and what had happened to poor Amber.

It was hard work, but slowly they made progress, and the wailing in the room became softer with each sleeping baby.

After what seemed like days, the last baby mushroom quieted down, and was tucked into its warm, comfy earth-bed. The five friends tiptoed away, finding a spot near the door that was the farthest from the beds, so as not to wake them back up. There they collapsed in five heaps onto the ground. They had never been so exhausted, nor as filthy, in their lives. Their clothes and hair were streaked with dirt and sweat, their fingernails caked to the quick with earth from tucking the babies in, and their wings were stiff and sore. They had never worked so hard, nor been so happy, as they were at that moment.

As their eyes met, and they saw for the first time just how dirty and disheveled they were, Astarte stifled a giggle. Then Saffron squealed, clapping her hand over her mouth to keep the noise down. One by one, they all collapsed into gales of silent laughter, hugging each other smiling apologetically.

"So that's what mushroom detail is," whispered Cerulia.

"That was quite a punishment," Vera added as she brushed a mud caked lock of hair from her face.

Rosalinda was smiling as well, as the fairies congratulated each other. Then, without warning, she broke down and sobbed.

"Rosalinda," cried Astarte, taking Rosalinda in her arms, "what is it?"

The pink fairy was racked with sobs, and unable to speak for a few moments. Then finally she managed to say one word.

"Amber."

All their smiles and pride in their accomplishment faded as they remembered their improvised potion and its disastrous results. Images from the vista-sphere flashed through their heads – Amber dancing wildly and flirting crazily with Eric. Amber knocking Robin down the stairs. Amber smashing the necklace on the ground, and the image going dark as the color drained from the Fairy Dust. Disaster.

"What did we do?" said Vera.

"What were we thinking?" said Cerulia.

"We were so selfish," said Saffron. "We made Amber do what we wanted her to do. We wanted to watch her fall in love. We never thought about whether she was ready to fall in love."

Astarte nodded. "And we decided that we knew better than all the books and all the teachers. I even brought out that stupid unicorn mane! I am so dumb."

"No, it's my fault," sobbed Rosalinda. "Me and my stupid pact! You were right, Cerulia."

"It's all our faults," said Cerulia firmly. "We're a team, and a team is supposed to work together, and play by the rules. We failed Madame Moonstone, we failed Amber, and we failed ourselves."

"But it's not over… it can't be!" cried Vera, getting to her feet and brushing back her curly brown hair. "We have to find a way to make it right. We've got to make her believe in us again!"

"That's just it, Vera," replied Cerulia. "We can't make her do anything. Just like we couldn't make these little mushroom babies go back to sleep. We had to figure out what they needed, and how each of us – working together with our own special talents - could give it to them. We have to do the same with Amber, if we ever get the chance."

"So that's what mushroom detail is? That's why we're here?" Rosalinda asked Cerulia, her eyes wide. A little smile began to form on her lips.

The five fairies looked at each other and nodded. Rosalinda was right.

A tiny sound, like the smallest of wind chimes in a light breeze, began to ring just outside the room. The sound began to grow with more and more notes sounding, creating a beautiful harmonious pattern, bright and vibrant and pure. It was a sound of water splashing in a brook, of stars twinkling in the night sky, the sound of bells and sunshine. The door opened and the sound came into the room.

It was Madame Moonstone. She was laughing.

chapter nine

# second chances

After washing and scrubbing away all the sweat and dirt from their bodies, faces and fingernails, cleaning and brushing their hair and wings, and putting on fresh clothes, Cerulia, Vera, Saffron, Rosalinda, and Astarte had been summoned back to the chamber outside Madame Moonstone's office where they had been given their true colors so many weeks before.

Astarte, of course, had used the occasion to completely change her look (but then, Astarte used any occasion to change her look).

Her red hair (that had before been in two pigtails) was brushed and pulled tightly into a single ponytail on the top of her head. She had replaced the skirt she was wearing with a pair of pants and balancing on her tiny nose were a tiny pair of glasses that human girls would assume had once belonged to a Barbie. Cerulia absent-mindedly smoothed her freshly washed hair, pushing it behind her ears and wondering if they all should have followed Astarte's lead in dressing more grown up. Saffron, who for weeks had forgotten to chew her fingernails, was at it again ferociously; even Vera, who could always be relied upon to stay calm, began humming anxiously to herself. Rosalinda darted quickly about the room, trying to come up with the right thing to say to Madame Moonstone when she arrived. Since they had left the mushroom beds, they had been given no hint by Madame Moonstone, Grock, or anybody else what would become of them next.

From time to time, the fairies would pass each other as they paced. Eyes would meet, hands would clasp, hugs would be given and received. Finally, without a word being said, they found themselves in a circle, holding each others' hands and trying to smile as they gazed at each of their companions. Minutes passed without a word being spoken.

Then Rosalinda, always the first to speak, uttered the words that they all had been thinking:

"I wish we could do it over again. Amber's recipe, I mean," said the pink fairy sadly. They all nodded and sighed.

"Do you think she's okay?" asked Saffron "How long has it been since…since it happened?"

"I can't tell at all," mused Cerulia, still playing with her hair. "It might have been yesterday, or a week ago. I can't figure out how long we were on Mushroom Detail. It's strange."

"Do you think they kicked her out of the play?" asked Astarte. "Or even kicked her out of school? That would be awful."

"Well, we know one thing for sure," said Vera, "she doesn't believe in us anymore." A single tear slowly rolled down her dark, smooth cheek.

"Nonsense," said a low melodious voice from the doorway. Five heads turned, and ten eyes stared in anxious dread. Madame Moonstone!

She opened her mouth, and once again the five fairies heard the extraordinary sound of her laughter – a sound made up of the tinkling of tiny bells, of bubbling water, of a spring breeze. Indeed, when you or I go into the woods, many of the sounds we hear are actually the voices of fairies, laughing and talking all around us. And Madame Moonstone's laughter is the most beautiful of all.

The fairies parted to allow Madame Moonstone into the center of their circle. They were confused – why should the Head Dustmaster be laughing? There had been no explanation when she came and gathered them up from the baby mushroom beds, and now she was laughing again! Wasn't Amber in trouble? Weren't they all in trouble? After all, they had broken so many rules, disobeyed their teacher, and were no longer believed in. How could any of this possibly be funny?

"Well, my dears," said Madame Moonstone, smiling a small, inscrutable smile, "I sent you away to find out what you must do to make things right. Do you have an answer for me?"

She expertly flicked a wing and spun around, looking each of the five fairies in the eye. The fairies looked at each other, not knowing what to say, or even who should reply. Madame Moonstone sensed their hesitation and rested her eyes on one of the five.

"Cerulia. What have you learned?"

Shy Cerulia, surprised at being asked to speak, looked fearfully at the other fairies. They smiled back and nodded, reassuring her and silently urging her to answer. Cerulia thought for a moment, then began.

"We're all really different, the five of us, and sometimes we don't get along at all," she said. "But we're also a team, and we take care of each other. I learned that when we work together, and respect each other's differences, we can really make a difference, like we did with the mushrooms. But when we fight and argue and show off and break the rules, then everything goes wrong, like with Amber. Is that right?"

Cerulia dropped her eyes, ashamed of the way they had treated Amber. Madame Moonstone nodded slightly, then turned to the next fairy.

"Saffron – tell me what you think."

Saffron quickly pulled her fingers out of her mouth and took a deep breath.

"We were selfish. We didn't really think about what Amber wanted. Just like when we were down with the mushrooms, we just screamed and shouted at each other and woke them all up. But when we stopped thinking about ourselves and cared about them, then we could really help and make a difference." Saffron looked up at Madame Moonstone, trying to gauge if her answer was right, and added sadly, "I wish we could do that with Amber."

"Thank you Saffron," said Madame Moonstone, who turned once again and faced another fairy. "Vera, what would you like to add?"

Vera had been fighting back tears while the others spoke. She looked around the circle at her four friends as the tears came.

"I learned that we have to take our time, and not try to make everything happen all at once. Like with Amber, we wanted her to have everything right away, whether it was the right thing for her or not. I think I learned to be patient, and take one step at a time."

Vera dropped her eyes, and wept quietly and Astarte put an arm around her shoulders to comfort her. But Madame Moonstone continued her inquiry, her eyes turned to the purple fairy.

"How about you, Astarte? Speak up."

"Oh Madame Moonstone!" Astarte gushed, as if she had been dying to unburden herself. "I was so dumb to put in the unicorn mane, especially when I didn't even know what it might do! I mean how stupid can you be?" Before Madame Moonstone could answer, she continued. "Fairy Dust fairies have been perfecting recipes for thousands of years, and then we come along and think we know more than all of you! If I've learned anything at all, I've learned that I still have a lot to learn!"

"Nicely put, Astarte." Finally, Madame Moonstone cast her eyes on the last of the five. "Rosalinda – you've always got something to say. What is your answer?"

Rosalinda thought hard, but thinking didn't seem to be working. Nothing that came into her head seemed to really matter. She closed her eyes and breathed deep. Then, slowly, she felt an idea come up, not from her head, but from someplace deep inside her.

"It's like – it only worked if we really meant it. If you just go through the motions it's no good at all! It's…it's just like what Astarte did just now – it came from her heart. I learned that if you want to make a difference, it has to come from your heart."

Rosalinda looked at Madame Moonstone and smiled. Madame Moonstone's face remained impassive, but her eyes were twinkling. She flicked a wing and faced each fairy again as she spoke.

"Well, well, well," she said, "what a lot of growing up you all have been doing! It's a shame you couldn't have learned all that before you put your little concoction together."

"Oh Madame Moonstone," cried Astarte. "We'd give anything to be able to take it back!"

"Really?" said the Dustmaster, with an odd tone in her voice. "Anything?"

"Oooh yes!" squealed Saffron. "If only Amber had never put it on!"

The fairies nodded vigorously but sadly. Madame Moonstone sighed an enormous sigh.

"Well, in that case…here."

Madame Moonstone flicked her wrist upward as she opened her hand, and a small, bright, silver object shot up into the air. It arced over the girls' heads, and came to rest in Astarte's outstretched hand. A length of fine silver chain, a beautiful silver winged fairy holding a vial of multicolored particles and, just barely visible, a strand of pure white hair. Astarte gasped as she realized…

"It's the Fairy Dust necklace!"

"That's not possible!" cried Cerulia as she peered at the familiar object glittering back at her.

"But Amber smashed it," said Saffron. "We saw her! She threw it away after...after she..."

Saffron was interrupted by the sound of Madame Moonstone's astonishing laughter. The girls stared open-mouthed at their teacher, who smiled and said simply, "You can't believe everything you see on the vista-sphere."

The five fairies looked at each other, speechless, then back at Madame Moonstone, who beamed a smile back at them. When she smiled, there was no doubt that she had been remarkably beautiful in her day.

Madame Moonstone continued, "You don't honestly think that I would allow you five to conjure up your own recipe– especially when you included a very powerful non-Fairy Dust item like unicorn mane - and actually give it to a poor unsuspecting human girl, do you?"

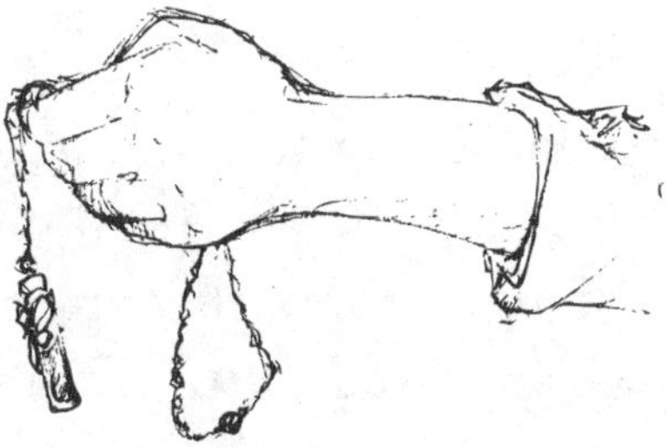

"But we did give it to her!" insisted Rosalinda. "We took a spinner to her school and put it in her locker. We saw it all!"

"Oh yes," said the unperturbed Dustmaster, "You did all that. But some of it didn't happen, just the same. Some of it is still waiting to happen."

Now Cerulia, who usually understood everything, gave a little frustrated whine. "Please, Madame, tell us what happened to Amber!"

"Be patient, Cerulia," replied Madame Moonstone. "Circle, please!"

The fairies snapped back into a perfect circle, desperate to hear. Madame Moonstone began.

"Well, you all had a fine time, basking in the success of your first recipe, lazing about watching Amber on the vista-sphere, feeling so pleased with yourselves. Then something new and exciting happened – something you couldn't resist."

She gestured to the ceiling and the vista-sphere immediately came to life. There were Amber and Robin! They were talking happily about that afternoon's rehearsal. Then another figure appeared. It was Eric Tolliver, who shyly said hello, and once again they heard Amber's flustered "Huuuu." Instantly they realized what they were seeing.

"It's the day we gave Amber the new recipe!" cried Astarte.

"Yes, Astarte. But please don't refer to that mess you created as a 'recipe'. More like a 'mutation' if you ask me!"

"Yes, Ma'am," said Astarte in a tiny voice.

"So," continued Madame Moonstone, "you all decided to have Amber fall in love, like she was a little doll that you could play with. What you wanted was not for Amber but for yourselves, so you would have something fun to watch on the vista-sphere."

She gestured again, and now the sphere was filled with images of...themselves! They were laughing and playing around as they filled a vial with multi-colored Fairy Dust, then inserted the tiny white unicorn hair into the mix. The five fairies looked away, deeply ashamed.

"You... you knew? You knew everything!" cried Vera.

"Of course," said Madame Moonstone. "As I told Grock that morning, the second recipe is where the danger lies for new Fairy Dust fairies. Do you think you five are the first to try to experiment after your first success?" She laughed again. "Trust me, my dears, what you did was awful, but I've seen much worse in my time."

"B-but what about Amber? I-I mean, it all still happened," said Rosalinda. "How can we..."

"Oh yes, Rosalinda, everything you've seen so far actually happened. You actually disobeyed me, you actually broke countless rules, and you actually put that poor girl in peril! You've done things that should get you expelled from the Fairy Dust Academy in two beats of a pixie's wings! But have you done actual harm to Amber? Mercy, no!"

Once again Madame Moonstone laughed as the circle of fairies stared at her in wide-eyed wonder.

"Oh, my dears," the silver-haired fairy continued gently, "you don't imagine I would allow that necklace to ever have gone around the neck of that poor human, do you? The necklace was removed from Amber's locker the instant you placed it there. The rest of it never happened."

"What?!?" the fairies cried out in astonishment.

"But we saw..." stammered Saffron.

The Dustmaster held up a hand, silencing them instantly. "What you saw is what would have happened if that necklace had actually been delivered. The necklace was removed, and the concoction was analyzed by the A.R.T.E."

"The what?" asked Astarte

"The Agency for Recipe Testing and Evaluation. The Agency is a group of forest gnomes who live underground just inside the Fairy Circle. They're very, very old and very, very wise. They can break down a recipe and provide a very accurate picture of what the consequences of any recipe will be. What you saw on the vista-sphere was the results of their test – the disastrous results, you might say."

"Then it was just a… a prediction? It wasn't real?" asked an astonished Cerulia.

"That's right. The A.R.T.E can create amazingly realistic projections of future events. Like I said, you can't believe everything you see on the vista-sphere!"

"But then, what actually happened that afternoon?" asked Vera breathlessly. "To Amber? And Eric? And Robin?"

"Wait! I know!" cried Astarte, her eyes wide with excitement. The shocked fairies stared at her as she turned and faced Madame Moonstone.

"It hasn't happened yet! Isn't that right?"

Madame Moonstone looked down at the little purple fairy. "Very good, Astarte. You are absolutely correct."

chapter ten

# fairy dust girls forever

Amber rushed down the hallway, flushed with fear and excitement. Since that morning, when Eric had talked with her and Robin, she had been in an utter tailspin. She couldn't even think about eating anything during lunch, even though it was pizza day and she loved pizza. Everything was a blur, and all she could think about was this afternoon's rehearsal, and seeing Eric again.

"You know Amber, you're a really good dancer," he had said. "Maybe we'll get a chance to dance together this afternoon."

To which she had answered "Huuuu!"

She blushed with embarrassment when she thought about it. And now, in just a few minutes, they would see each other again.

What would she say? What would she do? How did she look? She felt more alone and awkward than she had since her first days at the new school. Anxiously she clutched her Fairy Dust necklace, hoping that it would help her. But her faith in the Fairy Dust didn't seem to make her any less nervous. She felt shaky, even trembling, and for the first time, she wondered if the magic of the Fairy Dust might be wearing off. She missed the fairies. Would she ever see them again?

It was with these thoughts in her mind, and confusion beginning to take over her whole body, that she made her way to her locker to stash her books before the start of the afternoon's rehearsal. In her haste, she didn't even feel the gust of wind as it passed, or notice a few leaves and gum wrappers whirling around in a circle as she approached her locker. With ever-increasing anxiety, she tossed her books inside and was about to slam the door in frustration, when a beam of light reflected off something shiny, and she saw it.

There, once again, suspended on the hook, was another Fairy Dust necklace! Twinkling in the light at the end of the delicate chain, the little silver fairy guarding a vial full of brightly colored crystals. Amber took off her necklace and compared it to the new one. Immediately she could see that the colored dust was arranged differently and in different proportions – a new Fairy Dust recipe! And, if Amber had looked very close, she might have seen a slight bulge in her pencil box (it wasn't made to hold the five excited fairies that now were hiding inside it).

Without thinking twice, Amber took the new necklace, thrust it in her pocket, and left the old one hanging in her locker. She smiled for the first time since that morning and dashed off for the rehearsal, excited and hopeful.

"She's got it!"

The pencil case opened with a pop, and five different colors of fairy spilled out onto the floor of the locker.

"Whew," sighed Vera, "it's a good thing we all washed up after Mushroom Detail, or we would have suffocated in there!" The others giggled excitedly as they slipped through the vents in the locker door, and flew off down the hall after Amber.

"I can't believe we get to have a second chance!" said Rosalinda as they zipped along.

"It's Amber that gets the second chance," replied Cerulia. "I'm just glad Madame Moonstone is so smart."

"But I still don't get it," said Saffron. "I mean the whole time thing. How could it still be the same day as when we made the second recip… I mean, concoction? Astarte, how did you know?"

"Well, I didn't know, really," answered Astarte. "I just kinda imagined that time stood still. I didn't know you could actually do that!"

"But time kept going for us," said Saffron. "So how could it stop for Amber?"

"It didn't really," explained Cerulia. "If I understand it right, fairy time and human time are attached together, but they're not always the same. They can be unhooked from one another, so that one goes forward while the other doesn't until they're connected back again. Madame Moonstone unhooked fairy time at the moment we put the original necklace in Amber's locker, then rehooked it with just enough time left for us to put the new recipe in its place, and hide."

"Wow. That's a neat trick," said Vera. "I wish I could've unhooked time when we were studying for our Fairy Dust Final Exams!"

The five fairies giggled happily as they flew along. They were all incredibly excited to see how their new recipe – a real recipe – would change what they had seen in the vista-sphere. They couldn't wait to show that they had learned their lesson, and to see what would happen to Amber, Eric, and Robin this time!

They had been following just behind Amber as they flew along, high overhead. As they turned the corner into the hallway leading to the auditorium, Rosalinda looked down to find Amber. She wasn't there. Many of the students were hurrying into the auditorium, as the rehearsal was about to start, but Amber was nowhere to be seen!

"Where'd she go?" said Rosalinda. "She was right below us!"

"She must have gone inside. Come on!" called Vera, who flew on through the door of the auditorium. The others followed quickly, and they sped up to the folds of the curtain where they had hidden during Amber's audition.

The scene below was exactly how they had seen it in the vista-sphere: the stage full of pieces of half-finished scenery, including the staircase in the middle where Amber and Eric had danced – the staircase that Robin had fallen down. Mr. Conrad was sitting with his familiar scowl at the piano, kids were warming up, and Miss Jamison had not arrived yet. They recognized Robin, putting down her books and getting ready to climb the stairs to the stage. Surprisingly, Eric was there as well! He had come late when they had watched on the vista-sphere, but this time, there he was, sitting in the audience and talking to one of the other boys.

But no Amber.

The fairies were beginning to panic. How could they have lost her? Had the new Fairy Dust recipe made her invisible somehow? No, not possible. They had worked carefully, and Madame Moonstone had approved every step, every grain of Fairy Dust, every color. Besides, Fairy Dust couldn't do that.

At that moment Miss Jamison whirled into the room, just as she had before, and bounded up onto the stage with a smile.

"Helloooo, everyone!" she crowed, just as before. "Let's get started! We have a lot to learn this afternoon. Please take your positions where we left off yesterday."

Where was Amber?

Everyone scrambled into place. Robin took her position on the top of the stairs, only now she was looking for Amber as well.

"Robin doesn't know where she is either. This is awful!" cried Saffron.

Amber's absence hadn't been noticed by Miss Jamison yet. She went on exactly as she had on the vista-sphere.

"Perfect. Very good!" smiled Miss Jamison. "Now remember, this is a very swanky dance, and everybody is dressed in tuxedos and evening gowns. It's very romantic."

"Romantic," murmured a voice, a bit too loud. Only this time it wasn't Amber who said it – it was Eric! He was standing at the top of the stairs, staring at the open doorway.

"Ah, Amber, there you are!" said Miss Jamison. Everyone turned and looked, then stared, at the figure in the doorway.

It was Amber all right, but instead of her school uniform and her tight ponytail, she stood in a gorgeous floor length gown, with her hair piled artfully on top of her head. And around her neck, the beautiful silver Fairy Dust necklace hung gently. She was beautiful!

"Hello, Miss Jamison," said Amber softly and shyly. She stole a look at Eric, who was still staring at her with his mouth open and smiled a tiny smile.

The fairies, for the first time in their lives, were utterly speechless.

"Come on in, Amber! Let's have a look at you." chirped Miss Jamison. All eyes followed Amber as she walked slowly up onto the stage, then climbed the staircase to her place across from Robin.

"What happened to her?" whispered Astarte, high above the stage. "Did we do that?"

"Doesn't she look lovely?" cooed Miss Jamison. "I told you this was a romantic scene, didn't I? I managed to steal Miss Amber away on the way to rehearsal so she could try on her costume. Turn around, dear."

Amber turned slowly around. She was still in a daze. She had just put on her new Fairy Dust necklace when Miss Jamison appeared out of nowhere and took her to Mrs. Ramsey, the English teacher who was making the costumes for the show. And now here she was, feeling like a Homecoming Queen, in a lovely ball gown. She was deliriously excited, but managed to stay calm, even when she passed by Eric. "It must be the Fairy Dust," she thought. "Otherwise I'd be totally dizzy and do something stupid. Instead I feel like…like a lady."

"Very nice, very nice!" said Miss Jamison. "All right now," she clapped her hands, "let's get to work! Eric, please take your place between Amber and Robin. Let's dance!"

The rest of the rehearsal was the most fun Amber had ever had. Miss Jamison taught everyone the Finale, which was challenging and exciting to learn. Amber was able to dance the steps quickly, and from time to time would help out some of the others. Once, even Eric asked her to help him, and she found she was able to talk to him without stuttering or getting too dizzy, no matter how excited she felt. In one section, Miss Jamison had Amber and Eric dance together. He held her like she was made of porcelain, smiling shyly all the time, and only stepped on her toes twice. They hardly spoke to one another as they danced, but it was wonderful all the same.

"Look how grown-up she looks," sighed Vera, as she and the others watched from high above. "And how calm she seems!"

"She's so pretty in that dress. It's a good color for her," said Astarte, beaming.

"Maybe it's her true color," giggled Saffron. "I guess the Fairy Dust is really helping her grow a little. We certainly have," she added.

And so they had. The fairies' new recipe had more to do with poise and grace than it had to do with love and romance. Their experience had taught them that growing up happens one step at a time, and that they, like Amber, still had lots of growing up to do. They looked down fondly on their first human and hoped that they would be able to continue to guide her towards womanhood.

Below them, the rehearsal came to an end. Everyone was exhausted and happy.

"Wonderful work everyone!" beamed Miss Jamison. "We'll see you tomorrow afternoon." And off she swooped.

"Thanks for your help, Amber," said Eric, as he took her hand and helped her down the stairs. Amber felt dizzy and delighted as Eric held her hand, but managed not to faint.

"You're welcome, E-Eric," she replied. "You're really a good dancer once you know the steps."

"Well, I never would have learned them without you. See you tomorrow?" He grinned his big lopsided grin at her.

"See you tomorrow," Amber smiled back, and Eric ran off leaving her a bit breathless.

Amber looked around for Robin. She needed to talk to her. Robin had been acting strangely all afternoon. Earlier, as Amber had climbed the staircase in her ball gown, Robin had been beaming at her, smiling a huge smile. Then, all of a sudden, her look had changed to one of shock, like she had seen a bug crawling on Amber's neck or something. As they learned the dance, Robin didn't say a word (which was very unlike her), and kept staring at her oddly. At the end of the rehearsal, instead of leaving together as they always did, Robin rushed out of the auditorium while Amber was saying goodbye to Miss Jamison. Something was up.

Amber rushed out the door of the Auditorium, but Robin was nowhere to be seen. She dashed back to change back into her school clothes, then sadly made her way to her locker. Was Robin mad at her? Had she done something wrong?

"Amber?"

There she was! Robin was waiting for her near her locker. She had a curious look on her face - a look that Amber had never seen before. She didn't look mad exactly, but sort of anxious and jumpy. Amber couldn't tell what she was feeling, but she was relieved to see her.

"Robin, there you are! Are you okay? Are you mad at me?"

"I – I'm fine, really," Robin said nervously. "It's just... where did you get that?" she finally blurted out, pointing to Amber's neck. "That necklace?"

Amber gasped, and her hand jerked up and grabbed the Fairy Dust necklace. She didn't know what she should say. What could she say? Could she tell Robin about the fairies? Would Robin think she was crazy if she told her there were fairies in her locker?

But before Amber could say anything, Robin pulled something silver and shiny out of the top of her blouse – something she was wearing around her neck. When she took her hand away, Amber's eyes almost popped out of her head.

It was a Fairy Dust necklace!

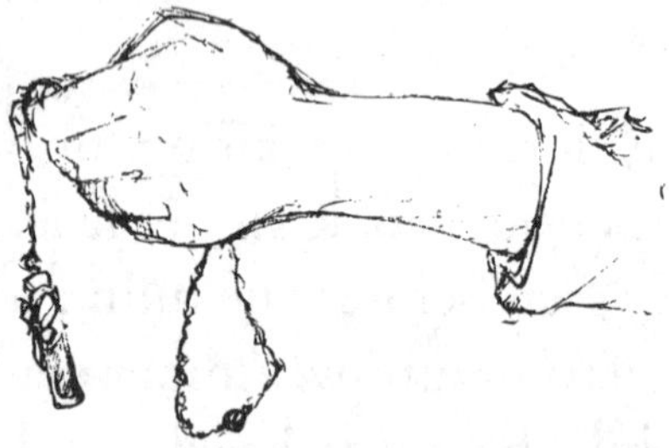

"I never noticed yours until you were wearing the ball gown at rehearsal today," said Robin quietly.

Amber was speechless. Her mind raced as she tried to think of something to say. Robin knew! She must know all about the fairies – she had her own necklace with her own Fairy Dust recipe! Did they appear in her locker too?

Then, without really planning to, Amber began to smile a little, mischievous smile. Robin stared at her curiously, then slowly she started to grin back. Both girls just stood, smiles growing larger and larger on their faces, until they couldn't stand it any longer. At the same moment, they burst out laughing, rushed together and hugged each other hard.

"We're Fairy Dust girls," whispered Amber. "Do you suppose there are more of us?"

"I imagine so. We'll just have to find them!" said Robin.

"But how did you… how did you meet your fairies?" asked Amber. She tried to think back to when she had met hers. It felt like so long ago now.

Robin smiled a huge smile at her friend. "It was the same day I met you, Amber! Let's walk home together and I'll tell you all about it."

Robin ran off to grab her books out of her locker. Amber watched her go, dazed but quietly happy. It had been quite a day – she had danced with a cute boy, worn a beautiful ball gown, and found a friend that she could share a secret with. What more could happen? She dreamily walked over to her locker, dialed the combination, and opened the door.

"Yay, Amber!" cheered five tiny voices, startling Amber out of her daydream.

"There you are! I've missed you so much!" cried Amber. The fairies were hovering in a perfect circle, as always. "I wish you were bigger, so I could hug you all!"

"Oh, we've missed you too!" gushed Saffron.

"But we've been, um, really busy," added Rosalinda, winking to the others.

"I love my new Fairy Dust necklace! I felt so… so grown up, this afternoon."

"We're so glad you like it," beamed Vera. "We worked extra hard on the recipe."

"And Robin is a Fairy Dust girl, too!" said Amber excitedly. "Did you make her necklace?"

"Oh, no, Amber," said Cerulia. "Fairy Dust fairies only take care of one girl at a time. She must have her own fairies."

"I want you to be with me forever," said Amber. "Can't you stay here with me?"

"We'll be here for you as long as you need us," said Astarte. "But there will come a time when you will outgrow us, and we will go on to help other girls."

"But right now, we're your Fairy Dust fairies!" said Rosalinda. "And we have something special for you – something you can use to call us again if you need us. Look in your pencil box."

Amber pulled out the long, slender box and opened it. She gave a little gasp as she spied something shiny and delicate. She reached in cautiously, and slowly pulled out a silver charm bracelet. As she held it up, Amber could see that there were five silver fairy charms. She looked closer, and saw…

"Why, they're you! They look just like you! This one is blue like you Cerulia, and this one is Saffon, with her blond hair…"

"That's right, Amber," said Rosalinda. "Our teacher, Madame Moonstone, made this especially for you. If you need us, just whisper into one of the fairy's ears, and we'll hear you, wherever we are!"

"Amber, you ready?" called Robin from down the hall.

"I gotta go," said Amber. She gazed at the beautiful bracelet shining in her hand, then at the fairies, her eyes becoming moist. "It's so beautiful. Thank you all so much!"

Amber slipped the bracelet onto her wrist – she couldn't wait to tell Robin all about it. She turned back to her open locker to say goodbye to the fairies, but her locker was empty. They had disappeared. Amber was startled for a second, then smiled, and raised the bracelet up to her mouth.

"Thank you," she whispered to the tiny fairy charms, then grabbed her books and scampered down the hall to meet Robin.

chapter eleven

# new friends, new adventures

When the spinner carrying the five fairies arrived back in the Magic Tree, Madame Moonstone and Grock were waiting for them.

"Well, my dears? How was your afternoon?" asked the Dustmaster with a sly smile on her face.

"Oh Madame Moonstone," cried Astarte. "It was wonderful. And Amber was beautiful!"

"The new recipe was just right," said Rosalinda. "Amber was able to handle all the excitement, and really enjoy it."

"And she got to be herself," added Astarte. "Not just what we wanted her to be!"

"And Robin has Fairy Dust fairies too. Who knew?" giggled Saffron "They're going to be such good friends!"

"How can we ever thank you?" said Cerulia.

"Well to start with, you can stick to approved recipes," said Madame Moonstone sternly. "I do not want to get into the habit of unhooking time to repair the damage you cause. Next time neither you nor your next poor needy human may be so lucky!"

"We understand," said Vera, still a bit ashamed. "And you won't have to do that again."

"I should hope not," replied Madame Moonstone. Then her face softened, and her eyes became kind and beautiful again. "Circle, please!"

The five friends arranged themselves around their teacher.

"You have all done well, my dears," she said. "Every group of Fairy Dust fairies has to discover what it means to grow up so that they can understand what Amber and others like her are going through. You have learned that lesson well, so I believe that it is time you moved to the next step in your training. Come with me – there are some friends of mine I'd like you to meet."

Madame Moonstone and Grock led the girls down a wide branch of the tree and entered a large round room. Grock closed the door behind them, leaving them alone with their teacher. The room was spotless with no furniture of any kind, and the wooden walls were highly polished. In the center of the room was a stand that held an enormous ball, which was revolving slowly. To you and me, it might seem to be like a huge globe of the world, spinning on its axis. But instead of countries and oceans, the ball shimmered with all the colors of the rainbow swirling across it. The colors made the surface of the ball come alive, as if the entire sphere was made of multicolored liquid. The girls had never seen anything like it before.

Once again, the fairies made a circle surrounding the colorful orb. With a flick of her wings, Madame Moonstone rose up so that she hovered overhead in the center of the room.

"It's beautiful, isn't it?" she said quietly. The girls were transfixed with wonder, watching the ever-changing face of the enormous ball. It was taller than any of them, even Saffron. "Step closer."

The fairies moved towards the ball until each girl hovered just inches away from the swirling surface. To their awestruck surprise, the colors on the ball seemed to react to their presence, and reflected their true colors back at them. All of the pink in the ball moved towards Rosalinda, while the blue knew to go to Cerulia, the yellow found Saffron, the green made its way to Vera, and the purple swirled over to Astarte. Clearly the ball knew they were there, and who they were!

"This is a Selection Sphere," said Madame Moonstone. "We use this for making many kinds of choices in the fairy world. I used it to select Amber as your first assignment in the human world, and again to select Mushroom Detail as your proper punishment. It has deep natural wisdom, deeper than even I can understand. As you can see, it has already correctly identified your true colors just by sensing your presence."

As Madame Moonstone spoke, the surface of the Selection Sphere had begun to move and swirl again. The colors came together to form images and pictures in front of each of the fairies – images that came out of their own minds and hearts. One by one the girls would gasp out loud as a picture from their own dreams would appear in front of them: Astarte saw herself in an endless closet full of gorgeous clothes, while Vera saw herself dancing gracefully on the top of a mushroom. Saffron blushed as she saw herself stuffing her mouth with pixie snacks, and Cerulia saw an image of herself looking very much like Madame Moonstone, standing in front of a class of eager young fairies. And Rosalinda stared wide-eyed as she saw herself transformed, wingless and earthbound, into a human girl!

Madame Moonstone smiled at her young students. "Yes, it knows everything about you, about your deepest dreams and desires. But don't be frightened or embarrassed, whatever your dream might be. Your dreams are part of what make you unique, and that is your gift to the world. But now, to work.

"From now on, each of you will have a partner, to help you and to keep you company on your new tasks. You have seen only a little of the human world so far, but as time goes by you will need to know much more. Your adventures are only beginning!

"The fairy world and the world of nature are very closely connected," she explained. "You have already studied the many ways which fairies and plants, like mushrooms and trees, interact with each other. But it is the animals in the world that are our dearest friends. Each of us has a special animal friend, just as we all have our true colors. Let me show you. Step back from the Selection Sphere, please."

They did as they were bidden, and instantly the sphere returned to its swirling patterns of color. Then Madame Moonstone approached the Selection Sphere, just as they had. As she did, strands of silver swirled in front of her, until the ball shone bright, and reflected the wise woman like a watery mirror. To their amazement, the image of their teacher slowly began to transform itself, becoming younger and younger, until an astonishingly beautiful fairy looked back at them, unmistakably Madame Moonstone as she had been years ago!

"Ah, yes, we all have our dreams," she smiled back at her younger self. Then, she raised her hand, and placed her palm on the surface of the ball. The image of the beautiful young fairy vanished, and was replaced by a view of the branches of a tall tree in the middle of the forest. Then, as they watched, a small speck appeared in the sky, and began moving towards the tree, growing larger as it came. Finally they could make out the large, soaring wings, sleek body and moon-shaped head of a beautiful grey owl that landed gracefully on a branch just next to Madame Moonstone's outstretched hand.

"This is Artemis. We have been together for many, many years now. Artemis, these are our newest Fairy Dust fairies." The grey owl looked at the awestruck fairies and nodded its head in their direction.

# *eleven • new friends, new adventures*

"He's beautiful," whispered Astarte.

"Can you talk to him?" asked Cerulia, bursting with curiosity.

"Does he understand what we're saying?" asked Vera.

"How far can he fly?" Saffron added.

"All in good time girls," Madame Moonstone replied. "Please stay focused. This next step is an important one for you to continue your training."

She turned towards the image of the creature beside her, and their eyes met. For several seconds they gazed at each other, as if they could read each other's minds. Then the owl nodded again, spread its great wings, and was gone. Madame Moonstone stepped away from the sphere, and once again it returned to its multicolored state.

"All right, my dears, it's your turn. Please take your places around the sphere."

The girls eagerly obeyed. The sphere, sensing their presence, separated into their true colors.

Madame Moonstone continued. "Now, clear your minds, and place your hand on the surface of the sphere. Soon you'll see what animal friend has been selected for you."

Five hands were raised, and five hands were carefully placed on the surface of the Selection Sphere.

"It tickles," giggled Saffron.

"Hush now, and concentrate," said Madame Moonstone sternly. "Watch and wait."

The five friends did as they were told, keeping their thoughts as clear as they could, though they were all bursting with excitement and anticipation. Slowly, in front of each girl, a picture began to materialize. Saffron was staring at a flowering bush; Cerulia found herself on the surface of the ocean; Vera was deep in the forest, in front of a rocky cave; Astarte looked out at the top of a grassy hill; and Rosalinda found herself gazing at a city street with lights that twinkled in the moonlight! Then, one by one, they saw something moving towards them until each girl was screaming with delight at what they saw.

On the bush in front of Saffron, a tiny bird, a thrush, had flown down and perched on a flowering branch.

Cerulia had been startled when the surface of the water broke, and she found herself eye-to-eye with a beautiful, smiling dolphin.

From out of the mouth of the cave, a playful bear cub came bounding up to Vera.

Astarte gasped, as a pony galloped into view, then came forward so that she could see the single horn in its forehead. It was not a pony, but a unicorn!

And up onto a fence in front of Rosalinda leapt a sleek, smoke-colored cat, preening its whiskers and smiling at the delighted girl.

Madame Moonstone had flitted behind each fairy, smiling her approval of each new friend.

"Well, don't be shy. Say hello!" she said. "Only don't say it out loud – just imagine what you'd like to say."

There was a moment of silence, as each fairy greeted her animal friend in her thoughts. Then, delighted shrieks came from all around the sphere, as their new friends answered them.

"We will have plenty of time for you to get acquainted, and you will learn all of the things your animal friends can do for you in the human world," said Madam Moonstone. "First ..."

Suddenly the door flew open, and the lurching figure of the goblin Grock rushed in, startling them all. "I'm so sorry to disturb you, Madame, but the alarm bells are going off again all over the human world! We're needed everywhere! What could be going on?"

Through the door the sound of the alarm bell could be heard, reminding the five friends of the fateful day when they received their true colors and got their first assignment – Amber.

Madame Moonstone sighed. "Ah well, it's one crisis after another in the human world! One of these days humans will find a better way to grow up, but in the meantime..."

"They have Fairy Dust fairies!" cried the five happy friends.

"Yes indeed," smiled the Dustmaster. "Now come along everyone. A new adventure awaits!"

She hurried off through the open door, and was quickly followed by flashes of yellow, pink, purple, green, and blue.

THE END